W9-BKP-014

PIZARRO and the CONQUEST OF THE INCAN EMPIRE
in World History

Titles *in World History*

PIZARRO and the CONQUEST OF THE INCAN EMPIRE
in World History

Richard Worth

Enslow Publishers, Inc.

40 Industrial Road
Box 398
Berkeley Heights, NJ 07922
USA

PO Box 38
Aldershot
Hants GU12 6BP
UK

http://www.enslow.com

Copyright © 2000 by Richard Worth

All rights reserved.

No part of this book may be reproduced by any means
without the written permission of the publisher.

Library of Congress Cataloging-in-Publication Data

Worth, Richard.
    Pizarro and the conquest of the Incan empire in world history / Richard
Worth.
       p. cm. — (In world history)
    Includes bibliographical references and index.
    Summary: Traces the history of the Spanish conquest of the Incas in
Peru, showing how they explored and then took over native cultures,
creating Spanish colonies in the New World.
    ISBN 0-7660-1396-0
    1. Peru—History—Conquest, 1522–1548 Juvenile literature.
2. Incas Juvenile literature. 3. Pizarro, Francisco, ca. 1475–1541 Juvenile
literature. [1. Peru—History—Conquest, 1522–1548. 2. Incas.
3. Indians of South America—Peru. 4. Pizarro, Francisco, ca. 1475–1541.]
I. Title. II. Series.
F3442 .W67   2000
985'.02—dc21
                                     99-39107
                                         CIP

Printed in the United States of America

10 9 8 7 6 5 4 3 2 1

To Our Readers: All Internet addresses in this book were active and appropriate
when we went to press. Any comments or suggestions can be sent by e-mail to
Comments@enslow.com or to the address on the back cover.

Illustration Credits: Corel Corporation, pp. 38, 40, 50, 116; Enslow
Publishers, Inc., pp. 21, 83, 112; Library of Congress, pp. 6, 8, 12, 16, 18,
20, 25, 27, 35, 44, 46, 55, 57, 59, 64, 72, 81, 96, 103, 117.

Cover Illustration: Library of Congress (Portrait—Francisco Pizarro);
© Digital Vision Ltd. (Background—Map).

Contents

Francisco Pizarro

Chapter 1

A Line in the Sand

Two sturdy sailing ships moved slowly along the western coast of South America in 1526. They were caravels—small vessels that curved upward in the prow and stern and carried light cannons for defense. The ships carried a hardy band of about 160 conquistadors, Spanish armed adventurers. They were looking for Indian villages that were rumored to contain rich treasures of gold and silver.[1] Atop each ship's mast flew a white flag with a red cross, the insignia of Spain. The conquistadors not only hoped to enrich themselves, but also intended to claim any lands they conquered for the Spanish king and to convert the Indians there to Christianity.

The captain of this expedition was a tall, bearded man named Francisco Pizarro. A hard-bitten veteran of many campaigns, Pizarro was already at least fifty. He was considered old in a profession where a sudden thrust from an enemy's sword or a bullet from a musket

Spanish vessels arrive in the Americas, to "discover" new territory for the Crown.

might rapidly end a man's life. Many soldiers never lived past thirty. But age had no effect on Pizarro's courage or his willingness to share the hardships of a long campaign with his men.

The ships dropped anchor along a promising stretch of coastline in the northern part of South America in what is now Ecuador. Pizarro's troops went ashore, hoping that they would soon find enormous riches. What awaited them instead was a small, deserted village. However, in the Indians' haste to escape the Spanish invaders, they had left behind some items of gold. The conquistadors had heard rumors of a great Indian empire farther to the east. There, they might discover a huge fortune in precious metals. Perhaps their dreams were about to come true.

Pizarro decided to remain in the area and continue exploring. He sent his ship's pilot, Bartholomew Ruiz, farther south to search for more gold. In the meantime, Pizarro's cocaptain, Diego de Almagro, sailed the other caravel back to Panama—a center of the new empire the Spanish were building in America. A grizzled old veteran, Almagro had lost an eye during one of his many campaigns against the Indians. On his return to Panama, he took the gold with him to show the Spanish governor there. His mission was to try to convince the governor to provide the expedition with the supplies it needed to keep going.

As Pizarro pushed inland, he hoped to find more signs of the fabled Indian empire. Instead, the conquistadors entered a harsh jungle. They found themselves waist-deep in thick swamps, fighting off poisonous insects and huge snakes. Ruiz was far more fortunate. He met Indians from prosperous villages who were wearing gold ornaments and beautifully made woolen clothes. Eventually, Ruiz rejoined Pizarro, bringing tales of his discoveries. Then Almagro returned with fresh supplies from Panama. The expedition was now ready to push onward. Pizarro believed that success awaited him if he could just keep going.

As the sails of the caravels unfurled, the conquistadors headed south along the coastline. Eventually, they spotted a large Indian village with at least two thousand houses laid out on long streets. Beyond the village stretched broad fields. There, the Indians had planted their crops. This was Atacames (located in present-day Ecuador). The conquistadors had no sooner anchored in the harbor when the ships were approached by a large army of Indians in canoes who seemed intent on preventing the Spaniards from landing. Although greatly outnumbered, Pizarro never lost heart. He led his men toward the shore, hoping that his steel armor and cavalry would make up for the men he lacked.

He was mistaken, however. Although the conquistadors reached the beaches, there were simply too many Indians opposing them. Pizarro turned back and boarded his ships, lucky to escape with his life.

Almagro and Pizarro decided that one of them should try to retain a foothold somewhere along the coast, while the other returned to Panama for reinforcements. The two old warriors did not trust each other. A heated argument broke out between them over who should go back and who should stay.

Pizarro accused Almagro of trying to avoid danger, saying,

> It is all very well . . . for you, who pass your time pleasantly enough, careering to and fro in your vessel, or snugly sheltered in a land of plenty at Panama; but it is quite another matter for those who stay behind to droop and die of hunger in the wilderness.[2]

Although Almagro finally agreed to remain behind, Pizarro decided that he would stay. While Almagro returned to Panama for reinforcements, Pizarro and some of his men retreated to a nearby island named Gallo to wait.

Unfortunately, they waited in vain. Instead of sending more men and supplies, the governor of Panama wanted Pizarro to return to Panama and give up his dreams of conquest. The governor sent two ships back to the island where Pizarro and his men were waiting and ordered them to get on board and sail back to Panama. When the ships arrived at the island, Pizarro's men were eager to go back. They had suffered terrible hardship and were nearing starvation. But Pizarro would hear none of it. He took out his sword and boldly drew a line on the sandy beach. Then he said to them: ". . . on that side [the south] are toil, hunger, nakedness, the drenching storm, desertion, and death; on this side, ease and pleasure. There lies Peru with its riches; here, Panama and its poverty. Choose. . . . For my part, I go to the south!"[3]

Francisco Pizarro dared his fellow conquistadors to remain with him to conquer Peru, despite great danger, by drawing a line in the sand with his sword.

Pizarro stepped over the line. But only thirteen men joined him. The others decided to go back to Panama. From this tiny group, however, Pizarro built a fighting force that would eventually conquer one of the world's greatest empires—the Inca of Peru. The Incan territory stretched for twenty-five hundred miles. The Inca would send great armies of fifty thousand soldiers against Pizarro and his conquistadors. Yet Pizarro would eventually figure out a way to defeat them.

Chapter 2

The Making of a Conquistador

Francisco Pizarro was born in Trujillo, a small city located in the Spanish kingdom of Castile, about 1471. He was the son of Gonzalo Pizarro, a veteran infantry colonel in the royal army. His mother was a peasant woman named Francisca Gonzales. His parents never married each other.

Francisco probably never attended school, and even as an adult, he could neither read nor write. During his early life, he tended pigs at a farm near Trujillo. Eventually, he joined the army and participated in the battles that drove the Arabs, known as Moors, from the Spanish peninsula.

During the seventh century, Moorish soldiers had streamed across the Mediterranean Sea from North Africa. In a short time, they had conquered almost the entire peninsula and established their capital at Córdoba on the Guadalquivir River in southern Spain. Under Moorish rule, Arabs, Jews, and Christians lived together harmoniously, creating brilliant literature, art, and architecture. But as their culture flourished, the military power of the Moors declined. Gradually, the Christian kingdoms that still remained in Spain reconquered the peninsula. They pushed the Moors into a small territory in the south. This was known as the Kingdom of Granada—seat of the famed Alhambra, the king's palace, which contained magnificent gardens, spacious courtyards, and beautifully tiled rooms.

During the last part of the fifteenth century, the Spanish decided to push the last of the Moors from the peninsula. The invasion of Granada was spearheaded by Spain's two most powerful rulers—Queen Isabella of Castile and King Ferdinand of Aragon, who had married each other in 1469. After a long, fierce struggle, the Moorish kingdom fell to the forces of Ferdinand and Isabella in January 1492.

Spain Expands Across the Atlantic

The year 1492 is famous for another event, as well. It marks the first voyage of Christopher

King Ferdinand, the king of Spain, encouraged trips of discovery to the Americas.

Columbus to America. Although Columbus was born in Genoa, Italy, he sailed under the Spanish flag. The great crusade against the Moors had unleashed a very powerful military spirit on the peninsula. Once Spain had been united under Ferdinand and Isabella, that crusading spirit was turned outward into conquests beyond the Spanish borders. Portugal had already led the way. Under the inspired direction of Prince Henry the Navigator, Portuguese explorers had sailed along the coast of Africa. Their explorations produced a rich trade in ivory, slaves, and gold. Eventually, the Portuguese would sail around the southern tip of Africa and open up new trade routes to the East Indies and India.

Columbus hoped to find a route to the East Indies by sailing west. He wanted to claim its fabled treasures of spices and precious metals for Spain. He also hoped to convert the people he found there to Christianity. Instead of landing in the Indies, however, Columbus bumped into the islands of the Caribbean Sea. He landed on one of them, which he called San Salvador. There, he encountered a group of people whom he called Indians—natives of the Indies. "I believe they would readily become Christians, for they seem to have no religion," he wrote.

> I investigated carefully to discover if they possessed gold. Noting that some had small pieces of this metal attached to holes in their noses, I extracted from them by signs the information that by traveling south . . . there might be found a monarch with vast quantities of gold, including huge vessels wrought from it.[1]

Queen Isabella of Spain, a devout Catholic, supported the efforts of explorers such as Columbus to win land in the Americas and to convert the natives to Christianity.

Columbus never did find this huge treasure. But tales that fabulous wealth could be found somewhere in this new world were told and retold by the men who sailed with Columbus. This inspired soldiers such as Francisco Pizarro to sail by the thousands to the Americas. There, they, too, hoped to conquer vast territories for their monarchs, find a treasure in gold, and convert the Indians there to the Catholic Church.

Pizarro's first expedition began in 1509. He sailed under the command of Alonso de Ojeda, who had accompanied Columbus on one of his voyages. In 1508, Ojeda was named governor of some of the Spanish territories along the northern coast of South

Source Document

Christopher Columbus, after discovering and conquering the said Islands and Continent in the said ocean, or any of them, shall be our Admiral of the said Islands and Continent you shall discover and conquer; and that you shall be our Admiral, Vice-Roy, and Governour in them. . . .[2]

King Ferdinand and Queen Isabella of Spain, who supported Christopher Columbus in his explorations of the New World, signed this statement, guaranteeing Columbus many rewards and privileges for his efforts.

Christopher Columbus was the first to claim territory in the New World for the Spanish, setting off a wave of European conquest.

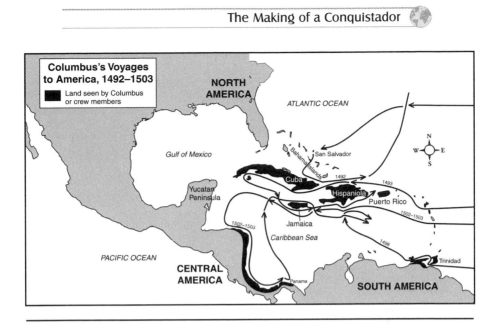

Columbus's Voyages to America, 1492–1503

Land seen by Columbus or crew members

NORTH AMERICA

ATLANTIC OCEAN

Gulf of Mexico

Bahama Islands

San Salvador

1492

1493

Cuba

Hispaniola

Puerto Rico

1502–1503

Yucatan Peninsula

1502–1503

Jamaica

Caribbean Sea

1498

PACIFIC OCEAN

CENTRAL AMERICA

Panama

Trinidad

SOUTH AMERICA

Christopher Columbus made the earliest European voyages of exploration in the New World, paving the way for future conquistadors such as Pizarro.

America. Ojeda's expedition took him to the harbor of Cartagena in present-day Colombia, where he landed. Accompanied by Pizarro and an army of about seventy men, the Spanish hoped to surprise a settlement of Indians at a village called Turbago. Finding it deserted, they spread out along the interior, searching for the Indians who were rumored to have gold. But the Indians outmatched Ojeda and his men. They surprised the Spaniards and killed almost all of them with poisoned arrows. Pizarro and Ojeda were lucky to escape. They would not have been rescued at all, had some of the men left aboard ship not found them and driven off the Indians. Eventually, Ojeda received reinforcements and took revenge on the Indians by slaughtering their families.[3]

Pizarro's First Command

In 1510, Ojeda continued his expeditions. He was accompanied by the bold Pizarro, who had not been scared off by almost losing his life a year earlier. Ojeda constructed a fort on the Gulf of Uraba along the Colombian coast. From this small fort, he led his soldiers against the local Indians, expecting to find their gold treasures. Instead, the Indians drove him back to the fort with their poisoned arrows. Reinforcements from Panama enabled Ojeda to keep the Indians at a distance, and he began to erect a town he called San Sebastian. But the tiny settlement had to face not only repeated Indian attacks but also the constant threat of famine. Eventually, Ojeda was forced to set sail to round up additional food supplies and reinforcements. Because he trusted Pizarro's leadership, Ojeda left him in charge of the tiny garrison with orders to hold out for two months. If Ojeda was unsuccessful in bringing relief, Pizarro was to abandon the settlement.

No relief arrived. After two months, Pizarro and his men sailed for Cartagena, a larger port town.

Pizarro and Balboa

After sailing into Cartagena, Pizarro met the convoy that was coming to relieve San Sebastian. The relief ships were commanded by Martín Fernandez d'Enciso. Under Enciso's leadership, Pizarro returned to San Sebastian only to discover that the fort had been destroyed by Indians. The new expedition was repeatedly attacked by the Indians, and Pizarro advised Enciso to return to Cartagena. When Enciso disagreed, a conflict broke out that almost ended in a duel between the two conquistadors. At this point, another member of the expedition, Vasco Núñez de Balboa, suggested that they start a new colony in an area he had visited some years earlier. He said the region was safe because "the Indians in that region [do not] use poisoned arrows."[4]

At Balboa's suggestion, the conquistadors sailed to another part of the Gulf of Uraba. There, they established the settlement of Santa Maria de la Antigua del Darien. Although Enciso became its first governor, he proved himself to be a poor leader. Eventually, a majority of his soldiers decided that Balboa should replace him. Pizarro became commander of the garrison. Enciso returned to Spain, where he plotted against Balboa at the Spanish court. A new governor was appointed to replace Balboa at Darien, and he was ordered to be put under arrest.

Before his replacement and arrest could happen, Balboa decided to leave the city. He took Pizarro and his soldiers with him. Balboa had heard stories of the fabled South Sea, which was supposed to lead to the East Indies. Traveling westward in 1513, he eventually neared the coast of Central America. Establishing a camp, Balboa took Pizarro and a few soldiers to the base of a hill. Then he went up alone and became the first white European to gaze on the Pacific Ocean. He called the other men to look at it with him, saying, "Behold the much desired ocean. . . . Behold! All ye men, who have shared such efforts. . . ."[5]

The entire company then proceeded down to the coastline. Balboa waded into the water, raised his sword, and proclaimed that the Pacific Ocean and all the shores it touched were now the territory of Spain. While he was in the area, Balboa also succeeded in maintaining peaceful relations with the Indians, who gave him a gift of more than two hundred beautiful pearls. They told him the pearls came from the oysters in the sea. Balboa set up a town called San Miguel. He hoped it would become a center for developing the pearl fisheries. These would not only enrich Balboa, but also, by sending part of this bounty of pearls back to the Spanish king, might help him win the king's support for more expeditions.

But events did not work out the way Balboa had planned. The king had appointed a new governor, named Pedro Arias de Avila, at Darien. When Balboa appeared to challenge the governor's authority, Avila ordered Balboa's arrest. Since Pizarro had been appointed captain of the governor's soldiers, he was given the distasteful job of arresting his old friend. Balboa was charged with treason, because he had illegally replaced Enciso. He was beheaded in 1517.

On September 11, 1513, Vasco Núñez de Balboa (standing in water holding sword) became the first European to view the Pacific Ocean from the Americas.

The Lure of Peru

During his expeditions with Balboa, Francisco Pizarro had heard tales of a fabulous empire to the south—the land of the Inca, where an enormous treasure in gold and silver was waiting for anyone courageous enough to take it. Balboa might have been the person to lead an expedition to find this treasure. Now that he was dead, there was no one Pizarro was prepared to follow into the Incan Empire. Eventually, he retired from the army. The Spanish government gave him a cattle ranch in present-day Panama for his services.

Meanwhile, incredible events were occurring to the north. In 1519, Hernando Cortés—a relative of Pizarro's—led a small group of conquistadors against the mighty Aztec Empire in Mexico. Cortés allied himself with some of the Indian tribes who had been conquered by the Aztec and held no love for their conquerors. With their support, Cortés succeeded in entering the Aztec capital of Tenochtitlán—a fabulous city of two hundred fifty thousand people, built on an island in the middle of a lake.

The Aztec leader Moctezuma, thinking the Spaniards might be gods, allowed himself to be captured by Cortés. Holding Moctezuma hostage, Cortés succeeded in keeping the Aztec under control and collecting an immense treasure in gold. As word of Cortés's exploits reached Pizarro, he may have wondered whether he might be fortunate enough to duplicate this same feat in Peru.

Hernando Cortés had accomplished the conquest of the Aztec in Mexico. Pizarro hoped to follow his example in Peru.

The First Expeditions

Pizarro apparently believed he could not undertake such an important expedition on his own. So he enlisted the aid of Diego de Almagro, a courageous soldier who had fought in the South American campaigns. Pizarro also had the help of Hernando de Luque, a highly respected Catholic priest who had the trust of wealthy Spaniards who might be willing to invest in the expedition. Pizarro lacked the money to finance it himself. Finally, he won the backing of Panama's governor, Pedro Arias de Avila, by offering to give him a share of any treasure he discovered.

Pizarro then set about preparing two ships and recruiting men to sail with him. By November 1524, he was ready to leave Panama in one of the ships and head southward. Unfortunately, it was already the rainy season, and the weather was very stormy for sailing. Pizarro's destination was a coastal area ruled by an Indian leader named Biru—after whom Peru may have been named. Almagro would follow in the other ship with more supplies and soldiers.[6]

Pizarro's first landings along the coast of South America were not very promising. As he explored a river that led inland, his men became mired in large snake-infested swamps. Continuing their journey along the coast, the Spanish ran out of food. They were fortunate to stumble across a deserted Indian town. There, they found some abandoned stores of food along with a few gold objects. The conquistadors did not linger here very long. They saw human

Source Document

Next morning, we came to a broad causeway and continued our march towards Iztapalapa. And when we saw all those cities and villages built in the water, and other great towns on dry land and that straight and level causeway leading to Mexico, we were astounded. These great towns and cues and buildings rising from the water, all made of stone, seemed like an enchanted vision from the tale of Amadis. Indeed, some of our soldiers asked whether it was not all a dream. . . . It was all so wonderful that I do not know how to describe this first glimpse of things never heard of, seen or dreamed of before.[7]

Bernal Diaz, one of the conquistadors with Hernando Cortés, described the Spaniards' awe of the Aztec culture as they entered Mexico City. Pizarro and his men would express similar awe when they encountered the Inca.

flesh being roasted over a fire—these Indians were cannibals.

Almagro never arrived with reinforcements, and Pizarro was finally forced to return to Panama. He had found very little gold, and his expedition had been a failure. Meanwhile, Almagro had been trying to find Pizarro. During his search, Almagro had found Indian villages where gold was a bit more plentiful. However, he lost his eye in a battle with the Indians. Thinking that Pizarro's ships had been lost at sea, Almagro returned to Panama.

The two soldiers were eventually reunited in Panama in 1525. Pizarro wanted to outfit another expedition immediately, but the governor opposed the idea. The first one had already cost the lives of some of his men, and the results had been meager. Eventually, the governor was persuaded to let Pizarro try again.

The Prize Seems to Grow Closer

In 1526, Pizarro and Almagro embarked on their second expedition. This adventure brought Pizarro to the island of Gallo, where he drew the famous line in the sand. Lacking food, Pizarro and his followers did not stay on Gallo for very long. They sailed in canoes to the nearby island of Gorgona, where game was far more plentiful. There, in 1527, Almagro eventually found them. He had convinced the governor to let him command a relief ship with a small group of soldiers.

Once again, the two conquistadors headed south—this time, to the Bay of Tumbez. Along the shore, they saw many thriving Indian villages like the one they had encountered at Atacames. Indian *balsas*—large rafts—came alongside the small Spanish ship. The balsas carried supplies of corn and potatoes, as well as an unusual animal called a llama, which was unknown to the Spaniards. An Indian nobleman, dressed in rich clothes and wearing such heavy gold ornaments in his ears that they had become deformed, brought peace offerings to Pizarro. He also suggested that Pizarro send a small delegation to shore.

What Pizarro's emissaries found there convinced them that they were getting closer to the great empire they had heard about in Peru. The Indian nobleman lived in a grand house where the Spanish emissaries saw much gold and silver. They were given a tour of an Indian temple decorated in gold. They also saw highly skilled craftsmen making gold and silver ornaments.

Pizarro's expedition was far too small to continue much farther. But his appetite for riches had increased, and if he could believe the Indians' reports, even greater wealth lay farther inland at the heart of the Incan Empire. Here lay not only treasure but also great cities, like the fortress city of Machu Picchu, high in the Andes Mountains. If Pizarro hoped to conquer this land, he would need many more troops. So he set sail for Panama, hoping to convince the new governor there to mount one final, large assault.

The governor, Pedro de los Rios, refused. "I have no desire to build up other provinces at the expense of my own, nor will I permit more lives to be thrown away than have already been sacrificed for a cheap display of gold and silver toys and a few Indian sheep," he told Pizarro.[8]

If Pizarro wanted to lead another expedition, he would have to go to Spain to convince the Spanish king to support it. So in 1528, he set sail from Panama, headed for the court of Charles V, who had come to the throne of Spain in 1516.

Chapter 3

The Incan Empire

Cuzco—in the language of the Inca, it means "the navel of the world." Located high in the Andes Mountains, more than eleven thousand feet above sea level, Cuzco was the capital of the Incan Empire. It lay at the center—the navel—of its far-flung territories.

According to Incan legend, the first Lord Inca—or ruler—Manco Capac and his wife, Mama Ocla, emerged from Lake Titicaca, the world's highest freshwater lake, which is located in the Andes. The sun god gave them a golden rod and told them to bury it in the place they wanted to settle. There, they were to begin a great Kingdom of the Sun. The location they chose was Cuzco, north of Lake Titicaca.

The Creation of the Incan Empire

During the early Inca period, spanning two and a half centuries from about 1200 to 1440, the Lord Inca gradually expanded their domain. They conquered the

Tiahuanaco, a tribe that lived around Lake Titicaca. From the Tiahuanaco, the Inca learned how to build huge walls and buildings by fitting together large stones without using cement or mortar. Since the Inca did not know about the wheel, they had neither carts to bring the heavy stones to a building site nor pulleys to lift them into place. Instead, they had to rely on sheer muscle power from teams of men working together to create these magnificent structures. The buildings lined the narrow streets of Cuzco. At the entrance to each building stood a door, shaped like a trapezoid and covered with animal skin to keep out the cold weather of the Andes.

During the fifteenth century, several great Incan rulers pushed the boundaries of the empire to their greatest extent. Viracocha Inca appointed governors in the conquered territories, establishing an administration for the empire. His successors—Pachacuti Inca Yupanqui and Topa Inca Yupanqui—increased the Incan territories until they became known among the Inca as the four quarters of the world. The empire stretched from present-day Ecuador in the north, southward into Chile, and from the shores of the Pacific in the west to what is now Argentina in the east.

During their conquests, the Inca took control of gold and silver mines. These yielded the vast treasures that were used to adorn the buildings in Cuzco. At the Lord Inca's palace, known as Cora Cora, the walls were covered in gold. The Lord Inca himself sat on a

Ruins of ancient buildings still demonstrate the architectural skill of the Incan people, hundreds of years after the fall of the empire.

golden stool to receive his subjects and ate his meals on golden plates.

Coricancha, the Temple of the Sun, was the richly decorated center of the Incan religion. Garcilaso de la Vega, who was born to a Spanish father and Incan mother in Cuzco during the sixteenth century, described Coricancha:

> All four walls of the temple were covered from top to bottom with plates and slabs of gold. Over . . . the high altar they had the image of the Sun on a gold plate twice the thickness of the rest of the wall-plates. . . . On both sides of the image of the Sun were the bodies of the dead kings in order of antiquity as children of the Sun and embalmed so that they appeared to be alive, though it is not known how this was done. They sat on golden chairs placed on the golden daises they had used. Their faces were towards the people.[1]

In the temple grounds, there was also a garden where all the flowers, trees, and animals were made out of gold and silver.

From Cuzco, each of the Incan kings had exercised power through four principal channels of control: administration, economic structure, religion, and the army.

Royal Administration

In the Kingdom of the Sun, supreme power lay with the Lord Inca. This position was hereditary. The oldest son usually assumed the position of king at the death of his father. The Lord Inca was a very active, involved ruler who did not believe in staying constantly in Cuzco, governing his people from afar. The Lord

Source Document

This Garden was in the Incas time a Garden of Silver and Gold, as they had in the Kings houses, where they had many sorts of Hearbes, Flowers, Plants, Trees, Beasts great and small, wilde, tame, Snakes, Lizards, Snailes, Butterflies, small and great Birds, each set in their place. . . . They had also in the house heapes of wood, all counterfeit of Gold and Silver, as they had in the house royall: likewise they had great statues of men and women, and children. . . . Like to this Temple of Cozco were others in many Provinces of that Kingdome, in which every Curaca indevoured according to his power to have such riches of Gold and Silver.[2]

Garcilaso de la Vega described the beauty and wealth of the Inca, which included huge gardens with flowers, trees, and animals built of silver and gold.

Inca regularly left the capital to make inspection tours that took him to the far reaches of his empire. He would stop at small villages, talk to peasants, and find out how fairly his laws were being administered.

Because the king could not be everywhere at once, he had to rely on administrators to help run the empire. From the nobility, he selected governors to run each of the large provinces. Smaller units of government, such as towns and cities, were run by Incan bureaucrats. But the Lord Inca realized that he could not always depend on these men, no matter how qualified they might seem, to be faithful to his rules and remain free

The Incan Empire, located in the rough terrain of the Andes Mountains, used unique systems of communication to keep even the farthest outreaches in touch with the government.

of corruption. So he relied on a network of royal inspectors—officials who roamed the countryside, checking up on the king's administrators and reporting back to the Lord Inca.

What made it possible for these inspectors to travel easily across the empire and for information to flow quickly back to Cuzco was a remarkable system of roadways. One road stretched along the Pacific coast from Tumbez for about twenty-five miles southward into Chile. The road covered miles of barren deserts between small villages set in fertile oases.

Another road—the so-called Royal Road—began north of present-day Quito, Ecuador, ran through the Andes to Cuzco, then ran southward beyond Lake Titicaca. The road was often eighteen-feet to twenty-five-feet wide as it crossed the broad plateaus that stretch between the Andes. As it went up the side of a steep hill, the road might become a narrow set of stone steps ascending for hundreds of feet.

Between the hills were deep valleys and mighty rivers that had to be crossed by the royal highway system. To solve this problem, the Inca built huge suspension bridges made of vines and reeds twisted together to form long ropes. Garcilaso de la Vega described one of the bridges along the Royal Highway:

> Three of the great ropes are used for the floor of the bridge, and the other two as handrails on either side. The floor ropes are overlaid with wood as thick as a man's arm, crossing the full width of the bridge. . . . It in turn is strewn with many boughs fixed in rows so as to give a firm footing. . . .[3]

These small roads lead to the Incan city of Machu Picchu.

Workmen living near each bridge made sure that it was always in good repair.

One of the primary purposes of the Incan highways was to support the royal messenger system that carried information from cities throughout the empire to the capital at Cuzco. Chasquis, as the messengers were called, lived in post houses along the roadway. A Spaniard, Pedro de Cieza de León, visited Peru in the sixteenth century. Cieza de León talked to the Inca and later wrote a history of the area. He explained how the messengers operated:

> When one approached the next post house, he began to call out to the men who were in it, and to say: "Start at once, and go to the next post house with news that so and so has happened, which such a Governor wishes to announce to the Inca." When the other runner heard what was shouted to him, he started with the utmost speed, while the runner who arrived went into the house to rest, and to eat and drink of what was always kept in store there. . . .[4]

To house visiting government officials who had to travel around the empire, inns were built every twelve to eighteen miles. Called *tampus*, the inns were supplied with abundant food and drink so a weary traveler could refresh himself before continuing on his journey.

The Inca never invented a written language, so most information had to be transmitted verbally. In addition, the Inca used a system called a *quipu* to keep certain records. This consisted of a series of strings and knots. The number and color of the strings, and the size and shape of the knots indicated certain statistics necessary to govern the country. According to Cieza de León, this information included the amount of tribute (tax) to be paid by each conquered territory, its population, and the number of poor people.[5]

The Economy of the Empire

The foundation of the Incan economy was a highly successful system of agriculture. Since much of the empire lay along the mountainous Andes, the Inca built long strips, called terraces, in which they planted their crops. Each terrace was bounded by a stone wall to catch water and keep it from flowing off the hillsides. The Inca also built aqueducts to bring water to their farmlands. In addition, they relied on fertilizers to produce abundant harvests. Garcilaso de la Vega explained that animal and human wastes were used as fertilizer in mountainous regions. Along the coast, the Inca collected bird droppings to enrich their fields.[6] The primary crop raised by the Inca was potatoes, which were used in stews and ground to make bread. The Inca also grew corn, beans, and tomatoes. Corn, tomatoes, and potatoes were introduced to Europe from the Americas by the Spanish.

Most of the people who lived in the Incan Empire were farmers. At about the age of nine, a young boy would begin learning to be a shepherd. He would become responsible for a small herd of llamas and alpacas. The llama was the primary beast of burden. It carried supplies along the royal highways. Alpacas

42

Source Document

[W]hen the Lord-Inca wished to learn what all the provinces between Cuzco and Chile, such a vast extension, were to contribute, he sent out . . . persons who enjoyed his confidence, who went from village to village observing the attire of the natives and their state of prosperity, and the fertility of the land, and whether they had flocks, or metals, or stores of food, or the other things which they valued and prized. After they had made a careful survey, they returned to report to the Inca about all this.[7]

Pedro de Cieza de León described the system of taxation in the Incan Empire, in which representatives of the Incan ruler first visited towns to determine the appropriate amount of tax owed.

The Inca used llamas as pack animals through the mountainous terrain of Peru.

were sheared for their wool, which was woven into cloth for garments. Young girls were taught by their mothers how to care for a household as well as how to make clothing and decorate it with embroidery and colorful paints and dyes.

All the land in the empire was owned by the Lord Inca. Plots were given out to people based on the size of their families. The people were responsible for working their own family plots. They also maintained the large fields that supported the local temple and its priests and the lands that provided food for the Lord Inca and his government officials. As historian Ruth Karen explained:

> The men of the village set out in a team, dressed in their holiday clothes, with music to pipe them to the field, and the priest waiting for them to offer his blessing. Work on the Inca's field was begun each year with the governor of the community symbolically turning the first piece of sod.[8]

Once the Lord Inca's fields were harvested, the surplus crops were stored in warehouses. If famine struck any part of the empire, or an earthquake created havoc in a village, the warehouses were opened and food was made available to the farmers. In addition to their other responsibilities, the Inca were expected to cultivate the lands of those who could not farm their own—widows, the elderly, and the handicapped. Each year, some of the men would be called away to provide service to the empire. Known as *mita*, this tax system might include serving in the army or maintaining the

Evidence of the Incan method of terrace farming can still be seen in areas of Peru today.

royal roads. While these men were away from the village, neighbors would maintain their fields so their families would not go hungry. "In an age when everywhere else in the world most men and women had cause to fear hunger, exposure, need in childhood and neglect in old age," wrote Ruth Karen, "the Kingdom of the Sun [gave] its subjects total security: physical, emotional and spiritual."[9]

The Religion of the Inca

The Inca worshiped the sun. The high priest of the empire was usually the Lord Inca's brother. The center of the religion was the magnificent temple in Cuzco, *Coricancha*, which means "the place of gold." Among the Inca, the most important celebration occurred on December 22. This is the date of the summer solstice, the longest day of the year (seasons are reversed in North and South America). Throughout the night, the Inca would pray to the sun and wait for it to rise in the morning. Then on December 22, the Lord Inca would offer a cup of wine to the sun god, and animals would be sacrificed to him. For three days, the Incan people would feast and celebrate in honor of the sun.

While Coricancha was the most sacred place in the empire, each city and village had its own temples maintained by local priests. These men understood the calendar, which was tied to the movements of the sun. They knew when the solstice occurred and could predict eclipses. They knew when the crops needed to be planted and the harvest begun. The priests also heard confessions from the local peasants and forgave their sins. In addition, they acted as seers. The Inca believed that the future could be told by looking at, or reading, the intestines of llamas that had been sacrificed to the sun god.

Women also played a role in the religious rituals of the empire. Each year, the most beautiful girls in the kingdom were selected to be Chosen Women. They received special education in the skills of weaving beautiful fabrics, making sumptuous meals, and participating in religious rites. Some of these women became wives of the Lord Inca or his most powerful nobles. Others became Virgins of the Sun and served in temples throughout the empire.

Defending the Empire: The Army

The Lord Inca was Commander in Chief of the empire's armies, but he often relied on his generals to lead troops into battle. As young men, the generals had been trained at a school in Cuzco. There, they learned military strategy and tactics as well as the history and culture of the Inca.

Most of the army was made up of common foot soldiers. These were peasants who served in the king's forces as part of their mita. Cavalry and guns were unknown in the empire. Instead, the infantry used large slings to hurl rocks at an advancing enemy. Some soldiers used a bow and arrow, and others carried six-foot-long lances. For hand-to-hand fighting, the soldiers relied on swords made of wood. Battle gear among the Inca was primitive. They wore wooden helmets, and armor of reinforced cotton cloth. Unfortunately, this would give them very little protection against the superior weapons and steel armor of the Spanish.

When compared with the other tribes they met in battle, however, the Inca were considered to be among the finest fighting forces in the region. To confront an enemy, an Incan army could move fairly rapidly along the empire's vast highway system. As the army advanced, it was supplied from storehouses full of the surplus food harvested from the Lord Inca's lands. Once the army approached an enemy's territory, its very presence might be enough to frighten an opposing tribe into submission. If not, a battle would begin.

In one of these battles, during the early fifteenth century, Viracocha Inca won a great victory that helped strengthen the empire against an opposing tribe. Garcilaso de la Vega wrote:

> As soon as day broke, they took up their arms and advanced against one another with a great noise of shouting and yelling and the sound of trumpets, drums, horns, and conches. Inca Viracocha insisted on leading his men and was the first to throw his weapon: a fierce fight then took place.[10]

The battle continued during the day until the enemy had been defeated.

After the Inca had conquered a new territory, many of the families who lived there were moved to

The ruins of the Incan city of Machu Picchu show the glory of the lost Incan Empire.

another, established region of the empire. As Pedro de Cieza de León explained:

> If it [a new territory] was cold, they were sent to a cold region, if warm, to a warm one, where they were given lands and houses such as those they had left. This was done . . . [so] that the natives might quickly understand how they must serve and behave themselves, and learn all that the older vassals understood concerning their duties, to be peaceful and quiet, not hasty to take up arms.[11]

The newly acquired province was then settled with families who had long been part of the empire. These families were given gifts of gold and silver for moving to a new territory. They stabilized the area and reported any unrest that might still exist among its natives. Nobles from the conquered tribes as well as their sons were often sent to Cuzco, as hostages, to keep a conquered people in line. These hostages were often educated in the Incan culture. They might learn Quechua—the Incan language—which was spoken by the empire's administrators and helped knit the diverse regions together. Thus, the Inca tried to absorb various cultures and create one unified empire.

The Rise of Atahualpa

When a Lord Inca died, the throne usually passed automatically to his oldest son, who received homage and loyalty from all Incan subjects. In 1525, Huayna Capac, the last great Incan ruler, died. Although the throne went to his oldest son, Huáscar, Huayna Capac had favored a younger son named Atahualpa.

Although Huáscar became king at Cuzco, Atahualpa remained in control of a large Incan army at Quito. Eventually, a civil war broke out between the two leaders. Huáscar controlled the capital, but Atahualpa had the loyalty of the empire's best generals. With their help, he defeated and captured Huáscar in a series of bloody battles. Atahualpa then took his revenge by slaughtering Huáscar's family and many of his followers. Huáscar himself remained in captivity.

The civil war, which occurred during the late 1520s and early 1530s, sharply divided the empire. It undermined the strength of the army and left Atahualpa in charge of a weakened realm. The Spanish conquistador Francisco Pizarro would exploit these conditions as he began his effort to conquer the vast Incan domain.

The Conquest Begins

If Pizarro had any hope of conquering the Inca, he and his two partners—the priest Hernando de Luque, and Diego de Almagro—would need the support of the Spanish government. Because they had already used all their funds on two previous expeditions, they were forced to borrow the money to pay for a voyage to Spain. Only one of them could afford to go, and Almagro believed it should be Pizarro. He was the most impressive leader of the three. But Father Luque was not so sure. He feared that Pizarro might not honestly represent all three of them in Spain and decide to steal the limelight, as well as the largest share of the riches, for himself. As Luque put it: "God grant, my children, that one of you may not defraud the other of his blessing!"[1]

Pizarro Recruits His Conquistadors

Nevertheless, in the spring of 1528, Pizarro set sail for Spain. No sooner had he arrived in his homeland, than he was thrown in jail by order of his old enemy, Martín Fernandez d'Enciso. Enciso charged that Pizarro still owed him some money from the Darien expedition many years earlier. But King Charles V ordered Pizarro's immediate release. Rumors of the rich Incan Empire had piqued Charles's interest. The conquistador continued his journey to the Spanish court at Toledo, in central Spain.

King Charles V ruled not only Spain but also territories in Austria, Germany, and Italy. To maintain this huge kingdom, Charles needed large sums of money. He had heard that Pizarro might be on the verge of discovering sources of gold and silver in South America. Charles wanted to learn more about the conquistador's explorations.

The king was not disappointed. Pizarro brought with him some gold and silver items captured from the Inca. He spoke of the hardships he had endured in his search for more treasure. He also told the king about the reliable reports he had received that great riches could be found farther inland. King Charles was inclined to give Pizarro his support. But the king was urgently needed in another part of his sprawling empire, so he left the final decision in the hands of his Council of the Indies. Unfortunately, the council took so long to make a decision Pizarro was finally forced to ask Queen Isabella—the wife of King Charles V— to help him.

On July 26, 1529, Isabella signed an agreement that proved extremely favorable to Pizarro. He would

Pizarro stands before King Charles V of Spain, seeking support before beginning his conquest of the Incan Empire.

become governor and captain-general of all the conquests in Peru, which was called New Castile. In addition, he would receive an annual salary of about thirty-five hundred dollars, a large sum for those days. By contrast, his two partners each received about half as much money. Almagro was named commander of only Tumbez, a tiny part of New Castile. Luque was made protector of the Indians, and he was promised a position as bishop, to come later. As part of the agreement, Pizarro was expected to take priests with him to convert the Indians to Christianity, and to raise a force of two hundred fifty soldiers to accompany him on the expedition.

Pizarro began his recruiting efforts in Trujillo, his birthplace. There, he was reunited with his half brothers: Francisco Martín de Alcántara and Gonzalo, Juan, and Hernando Pizarro. As historian Frank Shay explained: "Pizarro's original hope had been to enlist a body of gentlemen adventurers, each to supply his own arms, horse, munitions, and to contribute to the general expense. His brothers alone accepted these terms, sacrificing their small estates to secure funds."[2] In 1531, Pizarro sailed for Panama with fewer than the two hundred fifty men he was supposed to raise. But at least he had won the support of his family and the government of Spain.

Pizarro's Return to Panama

After being gone for so long, Pizarro was welcomed back by Almagro and Luque. They hoped he brought

Source Document

Charles V was very interested in establishing an empire throughout the New World. This page is from the first royal grant given by Charles V to Hernando Cortés.

good news. But what Almagro heard angered him. Pizarro had kept far more for himself, although he may have tried to convince King Charles to give more money and lands to Almagro and Luque. Nevertheless, Almagro felt betrayed and decided to lead his own expedition against the Inca. Father Luque realized that there would be enough money and supplies to mount only one effort against the huge Incan Empire. He convinced the hot-headed Almagro to change his mind. Pizarro assured Luque and Almagro that the three of them would divide any treasure they found equally. He promised to use his influence at the Spanish court to have Almagro appointed governor of some of the territory they would conquer.

With these problems resolved, Pizarro set sail for South America in January 1531. Accompanying him were one hundred eighty men, a few with cross bows and harquebuses (an early musket), and some horses. With this force, he hoped to conquer a mighty empire of about 12 million people.[3]

First Landings

Pizarro intended to return to Tumbez, where he had landed during his previous expedition. But stormy weather forced him to land farther north. After stumbling through a swampy coastal region, many of his soldiers wanted to return home. But Pizarro urged them to keep marching. He was now almost sixty years old. The example he set—a much older man who could

Only a few Spanish caravels, or ships, arrived in Peru to begin the conquest of the Incan Empire.

withstand the hardships of the climate—combined with the sheer force of his dynamic personality, convinced his followers to continue their journey south. Their efforts were rewarded. They reached a village that contained not only food supplies but gold, silver, and a large treasure in emeralds.

From here, Pizarro sailed to the Gulf of Guayaquil, a rich agricultural area where the Indians had planted sweet potatoes. He met with friendly Indians from a nearby island called Puna. They suggested that Pizarro rest his soldiers in their villages. During the civil war that had been raging in the Incan Empire, Puna's inhabitants had opposed the Indians at Tumbez, which was only a short distance away. When the Tumbez Indians heard that Pizarro was in the area, they came to Puna to see him. Friction developed between the Indians of Puna and the visitors from Tumbez. Pizarro feared the Puna Indians meant to destroy his expedition. As a result, he rounded up the Puna leaders and handed them over to his Tumbez allies, who promptly murdered them. The Puna village revolted. Greatly outnumbered, the conquistadors might have been massacred had it not been for their muskets, swords, armor, and cavalry.

Pizarro withdrew from Puna and headed toward Tumbez. Meanwhile, he had received reinforcements led by a young conquistador named Hernando de Soto. (De Soto would later explore the southern part of North America and become the first European to reach the Mississippi River.) With de Soto at his side,

Pizarro reached Tumbez, only to find it had been heavily damaged during the civil war. Leaving a few of his men to hold the area, he headed south. Along the way, Pizarro maintained friendly relations with the Indians he encountered. He found that the villagers welcomed him with presents of gold.

In 1532, Pizarro established a new settlement about one hundred miles from Tumbez. He named it San Miguel. He built a church, municipal buildings, and a stone fort. He also took stock of the treasure he had collected. The Spanish melted down the gold they had received and cast it into blocks called ingots. One fifth of the ingots were sent to the Spanish Crown. The rest was divided among the conquistadors, with the largest portion going to the expedition's leaders, including Pizarro and Almagro.

In Search of Atahualpa

Pizarro had recruited Indian interpreters to travel with him. Through them he learned that Atahualpa, leader of the Inca, was encamped with a huge army high in the Andes. How Pizarro expected to conquer such a force with his small contingent of men is not known. William Prescott, a nineteenth-century historian who wrote a history of Pizarro's expedition, believed that Pizarro was inspired by Cortés, who had defeated another large empire with a very small army of soldiers. "The brilliant achievements of his countrymen," Prescott wrote, "inspired him with confidence . . . and this confidence was one source of his success."[4]

Source Document

The representatives, inhabitants and citizens of this town have . . . asked us . . . to entreat Your Majesties on their behalf to order and provide a decree and letters patent in favor of Fernando Cortés, captain and chief justice of Your Royal Highnesses, so that he may govern us with justice until this land is conquered and pacified, and for as long as Your Majesties may see fit, knowing him to be a person well suited for such a position.[5]

Conquistador Hernando Cortés, whom Pizarro saw as a role model, wrote several letters from Mexico, where he had embarked upon the conquest of the Aztec Empire. Cortés's letters described his progress to the Spanish king and queen. This letter asks the king and queen to increase the powers given to Cortés in his mission.

Pizarro never seemed to doubt for a moment that he could do exactly what Hernando Cortés had done in conquering the native people of Mexico. Nor did Pizarro seem to show any fear in the face of such overwhelming odds. He also possessed the gift of eloquent speech. This enabled him to communicate his enthusiasm to the soldiers who would help him in his attempt to conquer the Inca. Pizarro demonstrated the power of his personality after his expedition had left San Miguel. Once again, some of his men were growing discouraged because they had not yet found the vast riches they had heard so much about. At this point, Pizarro delivered an impassioned speech. He said that any man who wanted to return to the safety of San Miguel was free to do so. He, however, was going on. According to historian Frank Shay, Pizarro said: "With the rest, be they many or few, who choose to take their chance with me, I will pursue this adventure to the end." Only seven men went back to San Miguel.[6]

Pizarro sent Hernando de Soto ahead with a small force to look for an Incan fortress that reportedly would get in the way of their march. With the rest of his soldiers, Pizarro headed toward the Andes Mountains. They had not proceeded very far when de Soto returned. He reported that he had, indeed, found a fortress, but that the Indians did not attack his soldiers. He also brought a messenger from Atahualpa. The messenger was the Incan king's brother Titu Atauchi. He carried gifts from Atahualpa as well as a message of peace for the Spanish conquistadors:

Hernando de Soto was one of the Spanish conquistadors who worked with Pizarro to conquer territory for Spain.

. . . I wish to be so bold as to beg you to do me the honor of granting three favors: first that you consider my Inca and King, Atahuallpa [the spelling of his name varies], your friend. . . . second, that you will pardon any offence that our people may have committed against you through ignorance or negligence. . . . and finally I beg you that the punishment of death you have executed on those of the island of Puna and of Tumbez and elsewhere . . . may not be repeated. . . .[7]

Garcilaso de la Vega, who wrote an authoritative history of the conquest during the sixteenth century, believed that King Atahualpa was afraid of Pizarro, even though his force was so small. According to de la Vega, the king believed that the conquistadors had been sent by the sun god. If this were the case, the Inca dared not do them any harm. In addition, there was a prophecy from the king's father, de la Vega explained, that a "people never before seen or imagined would enter his realms, depriving his children of their empire and destroying their idolatry. It seemed to King Atahuallpa that this prophecy was now being fulfilled. . . ."[8]

Perhaps this explains why the king did not send forces to ambush Pizarro as he began his climb into the Andes. The pathway the conquistadors followed was steep and extremely narrow. One false step might have sent them tumbling to their deaths in the valleys below. In this treacherous terrain, a small force might have destroyed Pizarro's army easily. But no force ever materialized to bar his way. Instead, Atahualpa waited in the valley of Cajamarca with a force of more than fifty thousand soldiers. Perhaps he believed that this large an army might be enough to frighten Pizarro away, without ever doing battle. Even if Atahualpa had decided to defy the prophecy and fight, he may have believed that fifty thousand soldiers would be enough to defeat Pizarro.

The Conquistadors Meet Atahualpa

Once Pizarro reached the plateaus of the high Andes, he rested his soldiers. Although it was summer in South America, the air at this high altitude was very cold. Once Pizarro had pitched camp, another messenger arrived from Atahualpa. He assured Pizarro that the king wanted to be his friend. Pizarro answered that he, too, hoped a lasting friendship could develop between the Spaniards and the Inca. He added: "My Emperor sent me to this country to bring its inhabitants to the knowledge of God and to allegiance to him."[9]

Pizarro and his troops then went into the valley that brought them to the town of Cajamarca. Francisco de Xeres, Pizarro's secretary, later wrote that about two thousand people lived in Cajamarca:

> The houses are more than two hundred paces in length, and very well built, being surrounded by strong walls, three times the height of a man. The roofs are covered with straw and wood, resting on the walls. The interiors are divided into eight rooms, much better built than any we had seen before . . . and each lodging is surrounded by its masonry wall with doorways, and has its fountain of water in an open court. . . .[10]

The Inca had erected an impressive temple to the sun god, and in one part of town lay a broad plaza enclosed by buildings. Guarding Cajamarca, a magnificent stone fortress stood on a hill.

When Pizarro entered Cajamarca on November 15, 1532, it was completely deserted. All the villagers had left to join the huge Indian encampment a short distance away. Pizarro decided to send a small contingent led by his brother Hernando Pizarro and de Soto along a broad causeway that crossed a river flowing in front of the Indian encampment. As they approached, the Spaniards saw the Incan tents with lances standing in front of them. Making their way through the camp, they noticed that, although some of the Inca were dressed for battle, they did not try to attack the Spanish conquistadors.

Instead, the Spanish were directed to Atahualpa's headquarters—a building in a large courtyard. There, they found the king surrounded by his royal household. De Soto told the king that they had come in peace. Then he invited Atahualpa to meet with Pizarro in Cajamarca. At first, the king said nothing. Then he answered: "Tell your captain that I am keeping a fast, which will end tomorrow morning. I will then visit him, with my chieftains."[11] After having some refreshments with the king and his noblemen, Hernando de Soto and Hernando Pizarro returned to Cajamarca.

Seeing so many Indians encamped on the plain in front of them, many of Pizarro's soldiers had begun to lose heart. How could they possibly defeat such a mighty army? Instead of gold and silver, they believed that only death now awaited them.

Nevertheless, Francisco Pizarro still believed that the Spaniards could succeed in defeating the Incan Empire. He began to develop a daring plan that just might bring them victory.

Chapter 5

Pizarro Lays a Trap

Francisco Pizarro's plan was as bold as it was simple. Like Cortés before him, he proposed to capture the Indian king. The Incan Empire was an absolute monarchy—all power flowed from the king. If Atahualpa were under the Spaniards' control, Pizarro reasoned, then he, Pizarro, could control the entire empire.

Pizarro Comes up With His Plan

But how could he capture Atahualpa? Pizarro could not march his tiny army out onto the plain and do battle with the Inca. There were far too many of them. They could easily surround his small force and crush it. In a small, confined space, however, Pizarro's meager forces, with their superior weapons, might easily destroy the Inca, who would not be able to use their superior numbers to any advantage.

The plaza at Cajamarca was the type of area Pizarro had in mind. On three sides of it were several buildings with large doors that opened onto the plaza. Pizarro decided to hide his cavalry inside the buildings under the command of his brother Hernando and Hernando de Soto. He hid the infantry in another building. The plaza was also guarded by a stone fortress, and on its ramparts he hid his musketeers. At a prearranged signal, the musketeers would begin firing at the Inca down in the plaza, while the infantry and cavalry charged. In the ensuing chaos, Pizarro would capture Atahualpa. On the morning of November 16, 1532, the Spanish priests who accompanied the expedition pronounced their blessing on the soldiers. Pizarro then positioned them for the ambush. There, they awaited the arrival of Atahualpa and his soldiers.

The king seemed in no hurry to begin his journey to Cajamarca. It was at least noon before the Incan Army began marching out of camp toward the city. Some of the nobles carried the king on a magnificent golden throne. A group of men ran ahead of the king, sweeping the causeway so the king's eyes would not have to see any debris. His soldiers moved slowly. It was almost sunset by the time they approached Cajamarca.

Atahualpa sent a messenger ahead to Pizarro, informing him that the Inca planned to camp outside the city that evening and enter the following morning. But Pizarro was anxious to spring his trap before darkness. His soldiers had already been in their hiding places most of the day. They wanted to strike. He sent a message back to Atahualpa, saying that he had prepared a sumptuous feast for the king and wanted to dine with him that evening.

Atahualpa decided to honor Pizarro's wishes. Leaving most of his army behind, he continued his journey into Cajamarca with only a small force of men who were not heavily armed. The king had no idea what awaited him. But he had heard about the power of the Spaniards' weapons. Why did he decide to leave most of his army behind and enter the city with only a small contingent of soldiers? "He was too absolute in his own empire easily to suspect [a trap]," wrote historian William H. Prescott, "and he probably could not comprehend the audacity with which a few men . . . meditated an assault on a powerful monarch in the midst of his victorious army."[1] In short, since no Inca would consider assaulting the king, Atahualpa could not imagine anyone else's doing it, especially when he was protected by such a large force. But he did not know Francisco Pizarro.

The Trap Is Sprung

As Atahualpa entered the town square at Cajamarca, his soldiers sang the joyous war songs of an invincible army. They had recently won a bloody civil war against the king's brother Huáscar, who had become their captive. Now they confidently expected to defeat the Spaniards and drive them from the empire. As the Inca looked around them, however, none of the

71

ATHABALIBA

ultimus Rex Peruanorum.

Atahualpa, the king of the Inca, became the first target of Pizarro's attempt to defeat the Incan Empire.

conquistadors seemed to be present anywhere. Indeed, Cajamarca seemed entirely deserted.

Suddenly, a robed priest appeared on the plaza, accompanied by his Indian interpreter, and walked toward the king. This was Father Vicente de Valverde, who had come to give the king a message from Pizarro. Father de Valverde delivered a long speech in which he asked Atahualpa to become the subject of King Charles V and pay him an annual tribute. In addition, the Incan ruler was expected to renounce his religion, accept Christianity, and recognize the authority of the pope. Otherwise, the Spaniards would destroy him.[2]

Pizarro probably realized that the Incan king would not accept the authority of the Spanish. Nevertheless, the Inca would be completely focused on Father de Valverde, allowing Pizarro to take them by surprise. As the priest withdrew from the square, Pizarro waved a white handkerchief. Suddenly, a shot rang out, breaking the silence. More musket fire followed from the ramparts of the fortress on the plaza. Incan soldiers groaned and crumpled to the ground. There was the thud of horses' hooves as the Spanish cavalry came charging into the square, followed by Pizarro's infantry. With swords and javelins, the conquistadors began hacking away at the Indians who were guarding their king. The Inca were unprepared for such an attack. Hundreds of them were massacred. Still, they would not leave the king unprotected. As one soldier fell, another would immediately take his place. A few were not so brave. They began to panic and run from the square, pursued by the Spanish cavalry, who mercilessly cut them down.

Meanwhile, it was growing dark. The conquistadors were afraid that Atahualpa might escape under cover of night. Some of them lunged toward the king, trying to kill him. Young Juan Pizarro, who accompanied the expedition and later wrote a history about it, explained that Francisco Pizarro prevented the king from being slain. "Let no one, who values his life, strike [him]," he said, reaching out to protect Atahualpa.[3] At this point, Pizarro received a cut on his hand, making him the only Spaniard wounded in the battle. Eventually, the king was toppled from his golden throne and taken inside one of the buildings on the square. Seeing their leader captured, the rest of the Inca began to flee. Without a king, the Inca had no direction and did not continue fighting.

The entire battle had taken about half an hour. It was enough to unseat a king and begin to take command of his empire.

The Looting Begins

That night, Atahualpa dined with Pizarro, not as his equal but as his captive. Nevertheless, the conquistador treated Atahualpa with the respect due to a king. Although he remained under house arrest at Cajamarca, Atahualpa lived in splendor. He continued to eat off golden plates, his court surrounded him, and the nobles who visited gave him the same respect and obedience as they did when he was in power. But nothing was really the same.

Pizarro had decided to spare the king's life so he could rule through him. Cortés had used a similar approach in Mexico. The conquistadors realized that the Indians would obey their own rulers. If the Spanish could control those rulers like puppets, they could rule a large empire with very few men.

While Atahualpa remained in Cajamarca, the Spaniards rounded up his warriors, who no longer had the will to resist, and looted his camp of all the gold and jewels they could find. But this was only a small treasure compared with what the Spaniards hoped to find.

Realizing that the Spaniards sought gold, Atahualpa decided to bribe Pizarro. He hoped to secure his own release by making an incredible offer. At first, the king offered to cover the floor of the room where he was living with gold. When Pizarro questioned the king's ability to gather that much gold, Atahualpa increased the offer. He stood on his tiptoes and extended his arm up the wall as far as he could. Then he proposed to fill the room—which was seventeen feet wide, twenty-two feet long, and nine feet high to the point the king had indicated—with gold. Pizarro, somewhat doubtful, agreed to let the king try. Atahualpa said that the gold would be collected in two months.[4]

When Huáscar heard that his brother had been captured and was offering a ransom to be released, he decided to use the same approach for his own release.

Huáscar offered to bring Pizarro an even larger treasure than the one Atahualpa had promised. Pizarro now saw an opportunity to increase his grip on the empire. He would bring Huáscar to Cajamarca and decide which of the two brothers should be the king. By playing the role of king maker, Pizarro would achieve even more power over the royal ruler.

When Atahualpa heard what Pizarro was planning, he resolved to avoid a contest for the crown. Perhaps he was afraid that the Spanish would select Huáscar as the new ruler. He immediately sent a message to the guards who were holding Huáscar captive, ordering that Huáscar be murdered. Huáscar was taken in chains to a nearby river and drowned.

A Fortune in Gold and Silver

Although Atahualpa was under the control of the Spaniards, his word was still law throughout the Incan Empire. Therefore, when he ordered that a treasure be sent to Cajamarca, his priests and government officials complied with his wishes. But it took time to gather the gold and silver and transport it along the royal roads. Pizarro began to grow distrustful of Atahualpa, thinking that he might not keep his word. There were also rumors of rebellions breaking out in the empire. Pizarro feared that the king might be trying to raise his subjects to fight the Spaniards.

Atahualpa tried to reassure Pizarro, saying, "Is not my life at your disposal? And what better security can you have for my fidelity?"[5]

Nevertheless, Pizarro sent his brother Hernando toward the area where the revolt was supposedly brewing. Along the way, Hernando and his soldiers fed themselves at the royal storehouses and stayed at the inns along the roads. Hernando Pizarro marveled at the Inca's engineering ability. "The royal road over the mountains is a thing worthy of being seen, because the ground is so rugged. Such beautiful roads could not, in truth, be found anywhere in Christendom," Hernando said.[6]

When Hernando reported to his brother that there were no rebellions, Pizarro was satisfied. He then sent Hernando farther east to Pachacamac, a coastal town where there was rumored to be a large treasure. Along the way, Hernando saw evidence of gold and silver being collected, according to Atahualpa's command. As Garcilaso de la Vega wrote:

> One day on the journey, as the Spaniards reached the top of a hill they saw that the side of another hill facing them on the road was all of gold. . . . When they reached it, they saw that it was jars and vats, and great and small pitchers, pots, braziers, shields, and many other objects made of gold and silver. . . .[7]

This was far more treasure than Hernando ever found at Pachacamac. Most of it had been hidden away by the priests who had not supported Atahualpa during the civil war with his brother. As Hernando and his cavalry returned east across the high Andes, the shoes on his horses' hooves began to wear out. Fortunately, he had collected enough gold and silver. It could be melted down and made into horseshoes by Inca who were traveling with them.

Back in Cajamarca, a large treasure had been delivered to pay the king's ransom. Although Pizarro was gratified to see such enormous riches, he now faced a new problem. His old partner, Almagro, had arrived at Cajamarca in February 1533, bringing welcome reinforcements. However, Almagro wanted something in return. He and his men had not been there long before they made it clear that they felt they were entitled to a share of the booty. Although these soldiers had not been there for the king's capture, they said, "we have taken our turn in mounting guard over him since his capture, have helped you to defend your treasures, and now give you the means of going forward and securing your conquests."[8]

Pizarro melted down most of the items that had been collected. As usual, one fifth went to the king in Spain. Hernando was selected to take this treasure to the king, along with some ornaments that had not been melted down. The rest was divided up among the conquerors, with the largest share going to the Pizarros and Hernando de Soto. Almagro and his men had to be content with a very small share.

The Death of Atahualpa

The king now demanded his freedom. But Pizarro hesitated to release him. He was afraid that Atahualpa would lead a revolt against the Spaniards. Already there were more rumors of rebellions, and Pizarro had sent de Soto with a contingent of soldiers to investigate. De Soto and Hernando Pizarro had become friendly with Atahualpa during his captivity. They believed that, even if the king were not released, his life should be safeguarded. Without the presence of Hernando and de Soto at Cajamarca, there was no one to speak up for the king. Meanwhile, a majority of the Spanish conquistadors, including Almagro, believed that Atahualpa should be put to death. Alive, he would become a rallying point for the Inca. At a word from Atahualpa, they might rise in rebellion, killing all the Spaniards.

Pizarro and Almagro decided to hold a trial at which Atahualpa would be charged with a list of serious offenses. Among these were taking the throne from his brother, having Huáscar murdered, and trying to start uprisings against the Spanish. Of course, the trial was a sham: The decision was never in doubt. Atahualpa was found guilty. On the evening of August 29, 1533, he was taken from his rooms and garroted—strangled by an iron collar, which was tightened around his neck until he died. He was buried at the church of San Francisco, which Pizarro had built in Cajamarca with some of the treasure collected from the Inca.

Now that he had been reinforced by Almagro and his men, Pizarro decided to advance toward Cuzco. At first, the Inca did not harass his army. But as Pizarro approached the town of Xauxa, an army of Indians had drawn itself up along the banks of a broad river.

The bridge destroyed, the Spaniards began crossing the stream on their horses. The Indians were so surprised that the conquistadors would try to cross, they fled. Pizarro entered Xauxa and established his own fortress.

Meanwhile, he sent de Soto to scout ahead and report back any signs of the enemy on the road to Cuzco. As de Soto entered some rocky areas, he was ambushed by the Inca, who were lying in wait for him. The Inca attacked, killing a few of his soldiers. Gradually, de Soto succeeded in forcing them to retreat, until both armies found themselves on open ground. As night fell, the soldiers rested on the battlefield. Fortunately, de Soto had been sending messages to Pizarro during his scouting expedition, saying that he had seen signs of the enemy. Taking no chances, Pizarro ordered Almagro forward with reinforcements. He reached de Soto while his troops were camped for the night. The next morning, when the Inca saw that the Spanish Army had increased in size, they retreated.

The Spaniards Enter Cuzco

Before making his final advance into Cuzco, Pizarro left Xauxa to join the advance guard under Almagro and de Soto. Along the way, he was attacked by a force of six thousand Inca under the command of Atahualpa's brother Titu Atauchi. Although a few Spaniards were killed in the encounter, Pizarro escaped and united his troops with the advance guard.

Pizarro made a dramatic entrance into the city of Cuzco to demonstrate his conquest of the Incan Empire.

Then they marched to Cuzco. The conquistadors entered the city in three columns on November 15, 1533. From Cajamarca to Cuzco, the Spaniards had journeyed six hundred miles.

Pizarro's success, however, would not have been possible without help from some of the Inca themselves. The civil war between Huáscar and Atahualpa had divided the Inca. As historian Edwin Williamson wrote, Pizarro's

> murder of Atahuallpa was welcomed by Huáscar's branch of the Inca royal family, who began to collaborate with the Spaniards in the hope of regaining the throne. . . . Pizarro naturally seized this chance to present himself to the tribes loyal to Huáscar as the restorer of the legitimate Inca line.

Thus, when the Spaniards arrived in Cuzco, they were seen as "liberators" who were driving out the forces loyal to Atahualpa.[9]

One of Pizarro's first acts after settling down in Cuzco was to appoint a new king. He realized that the Spaniards alone could not control the empire. They needed a puppet monarch to whom the Inca could swear allegiance. Prince Manco, brother of Huáscar, had approached Pizarro. He said that he was willing to rule under the Spaniards. Early in 1534, with Pizarro's troops and the Incan nobles present in the great square of Cuzco, Manco was coronated. Placing the *borla*, or crown of office, on Manco's head, was Pizarro, symbolizing his role as king maker.[10]

The Spanish Crown claimed a great deal of territory in the Americas, especially after the defeat of the Aztec Empire in Mexico and the Incan Empire in Peru.

Although Pizarro had tried to prevent looting in Cuzco, his soldiers, believing that vast riches lay in the capital, could not be controlled. They rampaged throughout the city. They took gold and jewels from the palaces of the kings, stealing whatever they could carry from the homes of the nobility. They dug up the dead who were buried with their jewels, and even tortured some of the local citizens to find out where they had hidden their valuables.

The conquistadors may have believed that the war was now over and that they could do whatever they wanted. The Spaniards would soon discover they were greatly mistaken.

Civil War

Beating the Inca was one thing, but controlling their empire was something else. After Pizarro entered Cuzco, he faced two difficult enemies. The Spaniards themselves fought over the division of the spoils. There were also the Inca, who hoped that infighting would weaken the Spanish and waited for another Incan leader who could then bring them victory against the invaders.

Francisco Pizarro realized that he could not rule the Incan domain by himself. Manco might eventually help him win the allegiance of the Indians. But Pizarro also needed a group of trusted Spanish lieutenants to help him maintain control of so vast an empire.

Fortunately, the old conquistador had his younger half brothers. He created a new government in Cuzco, with Juan and Gonzalo Pizarro among its chief officials. Hernando was still in Spain, but when he returned, he would assume a position of leadership in the new colony, too.

In addition to taking over the government, Pizarro hoped to win over the souls of the Indians to the Catholic Church. Father Vicente de Valverde, who had been with Pizarro at Cajamarca, became bishop of Cuzco. He led Spanish efforts to eliminate the Incan religion and replace it with Catholicism. The Incan temples were destroyed, and on the central square in Cuzco a new Catholic cathedral was erected. Spanish missionaries were also arriving in Peru. They began converting the Indians to Christianity.

While Pizarro was dealing with the internal affairs of the empire, a serious external threat arose to challenge his leadership. Pedro de Alvarado, the Spanish governor of Guatemala, had heard about the vast riches of the Incan Empire and wanted some of them for himself. A veteran of the campaign against the Aztec in Mexico, Alvarado hoped to repeat this triumph in Peru. He led his invasion force toward Quito, where a large treasure was reportedly stored. Unfortunately, Alvarado followed a route that took him through the high Andes. Unfamiliar with the terrain, he got lost. Some of his soldiers froze to death in the terrible cold. By the time Alvarado approached Quito, Pizarro had already received reports of his invasion and sent Diego de Almagro west to oppose him.

As the two armies approached each other, Almagro decided that a bribe might be better than a battle. He met Alvarado and offered to pay him for his expenses if he would call off the invasion and let his troops join Almagro's forces. Alvarado agreed. He had become convinced that no treasure lay in Quito. Meanwhile, Almagro's own men had persuaded Alvarado's troops that a large store of treasure did lie to the east at Cuzco. As a result, conflict was avoided and the invasion came to an end.[1] Almagro had saved Pizarro's conquests without firing a shot—but it was the last time the two leaders would work together.

Battles for Control

In the meantime, Pizarro left Cuzco and headed west. After meeting briefly with Alvarado before his return to Guatemala, Pizarro began exploring the coast for a site on which to establish a new city. Pizarro realized that he needed a location that could easily be supplied from Spain. Cuzco was too far inland and could be reached only by narrow roads winding through the Andes.

On January 6, 1535, Pizarro established his new settlement a few miles from the coast on a river that flowed into the Pacific Ocean. Pizarro called it the City of Kings. It would later be known as Lima, after an Indian name for the area. He intended to make this city the showpiece of his new colony. He designed it with broad streets, beautiful gardens, and a spacious plaza flanked by an impressive cathedral and a palace for the governor. Pizarro hoped to attract shiploads of colonists from Spain, who would live in Lima and establish permanent homes in Peru. Pizarro saw himself not only as a conquistador in search of large sums of gold and silver but also as the founder of a great Spanish colony that would live on long after his death.

Indeed, Charles V was delighted when he heard about the conquest of Peru. He sent word that the territory under Pizarro's rule had been enlarged by another two hundred miles, making the colony even grander. At the same time, Almagro had been given his own piece of land to govern. It stretched from the Peruvian border six hundred miles southward. Unfortunately, Almagro and Pizarro disagreed on where one colony ended and the other began. Almagro believed that his territory included Cuzco, and he challenged Pizarro's brothers for control of the city. As a conflict erupted in Cuzco, Pizarro was forced to leave Lima to mediate this dispute. He finally convinced Almagro that he should explore the new land he had been given—which included the modern nation of Chile—because he might find large stores of gold hidden there.

The conflict between Pizarro and Almagro had not gone unnoticed by Manco, the new Incan king. Manco realized that his position gave him no authority to prevent the Spaniards from mistreating the Incan people. He could only change conditions in the empire by leading a revolt that would drive out the invaders. But for that revolt to begin, Manco would have to escape from the Spaniards at Cuzco, who watched him constantly. The king finally convinced Hernando Pizarro that a magnificent gold statue lay hidden in a secret place. With an escort of only two Spanish soldiers, the king was permitted to retrieve it. Once outside the Cuzco city limits, Manco slipped away from his guards and disappeared.

The Inca Revolt

The king then began to gather an army. Messengers sped along the royal highways, each stretch of which was named after one of Manco's royal ancestors. They announced that the king had left Cuzco and intended to lead a rebellion against the Spaniards. As Incan warriors gathered around the king, Juan Pizarro led a small force of conquistadors to find Manco and bring him back to Cuzco. Instead, he found a large Incan army on the other side of a river. Pedro Pizarro, who accompanied his cousin, later explained what Juan did next:

> [He] ordered all of us to throw ourselves into the river and swim across it with our horses, and, with him doing so . . . first, we all followed him, and thus we crossed the river by swimming and attacked [them] . . . and routed them, and the Indians withdrew to some high peaks toward the mountains where the horses could not climb up.[2]

Finally, Juan was ordered by his brother Hernando to return to the city. There, he found Cuzco surrounded by an army of Incan soldiers. The Incan force was led by Manco, who had put the capital under siege. The siege would last for more than six months—from February to August 1536.

Manco allowed Juan and his soldiers to return into Cuzco. But these reinforcements gave the Spaniards an army of only two hundred fighting men. Fortunately, they had the help of one thousand Indian allies—the Canari, whose people had been slaughtered by Atahualpa and bore no love for the Inca.[3] Outside the city lay an enormous force of Incan soldiers whose campfires at night "lookcd like nothing other than a very serene sky full of stars."[4]

During the day, the Inca continued their assault on the city. They shot burning arrows into the houses of Cuzco, setting their thatched roofs and wooden beams on fire. As a result, the Spaniards were forced to camp in the large central plaza. From this position, Hernando led attacks against the Inca, who advanced into the outer limits of Cuzco. As soon as the Spanish cavalry cleared the Inca out of one neighborhood, the Inca returned and set up barricades to prevent the horses from moving down the streets. Although the Inca lost many men in this house-to-house fighting, they did not give up the siege.

Guarding the city was a huge stone fortress called Sacsahuaman. The Inca had captured the fort, giving them a strong defensive position against the Spaniards. It was surrounded by several thick walls, making an assault extremely difficult. Nevertheless, Hernando and Juan Pizarro decided that the fortress must be cleared of Inca if the Spaniards were to regain control of Cuzco and the surrounding area.

One night, Juan led a group of conquistadors toward the entrance of the outer wall, which had been blockaded by rocks. They removed the stones and streamed through the entrance. Although they met a fierce attack by the Inca, Juan and his men successfully stormed the second wall. They entered an inner courtyard at the foot of large towers that formed part of the giant fortress. At this point, Juan was struck on the head by a large rock that was thrown by one of the Inca. Juan was fatally wounded.

His brother Hernando then took up the assault against the towers. The Inca were running out of water, and in their desperation, some jumped to their deaths from the towers. Others surrendered. Using long scaling ladders, the Spaniards eventually succeeded in entering the towers and killing many of the Incan defenders. Only their leader continued fighting. He would not surrender. Instead, he jumped from the tower and killed himself.[5]

The siege continued. The Spaniards soon found themselves running extremely short of supplies. Since the Inca were defending most of the passes through the mountains, Francisco Pizarro could not send any reinforcements to his brothers in Cuzco. The Inca had also attacked Lima and other Spanish settlements, beheading some of the Spanish settlers and rolling their heads into the plaza at Cuzco.[6]

Unknown to the Spaniards, however, time was on their side. Supplies were running short for the Inca, and in August, they had to plant their crops for the coming year. Manco had little choice but to send many of his warriors home to their farms. With the lifting of the siege, he retreated to a heavily defended stronghold on a hill. Hoping to catch Manco by surprise, Hernando Pizarro led an army from Cuzco to attack at dawn. Instead, it was Pizarro's forces who were surprised, encountering withering fire from the Indians who had been waiting for them. Pizarro was forced to retreat, leaving Manco secure inside his fortress.

The Return of Almagro

Soon after Hernando Pizarro's encounter with Manco, he was forced to deal with a new threat. Diego de Almagro had led his men on a harrowing journey through the Andes into Chile. Hoping to find a treasure in gold equal to the one his partner, Pizarro, had discovered, Almagro instead found nothing. Unwilling to return to Peru over the same route through the Andes, Almagro decided to travel along the coast. There, he entered the Atacama Desert, where his men were forced to withstand terrible heat and thirst on their march north.

After failing in his expedition to Chile, Almagro now decided to take control of the city that he had claimed in the past—Cuzco. Of course, Hernando Pizarro had no intention of giving up the capital, especially to a man he disliked as much as the one-eyed Almagro. Meanwhile, Francisco Pizarro was sending reinforcements over the mountains to his brother to strengthen the Pizarros' hold on Cuzco. When

Almagro realized that reinforcements were on the way, he knew that his army had to act quickly. On the night of April 8, 1537, Almagro's troops slipped into the city under cover of darkness. His cavalry quickly blocked all the main streets and surrounded the house where Hernando and his brother Gonzalo were staying. Under the direction of Almagro's most trusted commander, Rodrigo de Orgonez, the invading forces tried to force their way into the house, but it was heavily defended. Finally, Orgonez decided to set fire to it. Hernando and Gonzalo Pizarro surrendered just before the building collapsed.[7]

Pizarro and Almagro Battle for Control

With the two Pizarros safely imprisoned in Cuzco, Almagro was now in the strongest position he had ever held since landing in Peru. Orgonez urged him to take advantage of the situation and execute the Pizarros. He warned Almagro that "a Pizarro was never known to forget an injury."[8] In other words, if he did not act, he might live to regret it. But Almagro was apparently too busy dealing with another problem.

The relief force sent by Francisco Pizarro was approaching Cuzco. Almagro immediately sent out messengers. They informed the relief column that Almagro was now in control of the capital and that they should acknowledge his authority. But their commanding general, Alonso de Alvarado, refused. Instead, he drew up his army in front of a river, taking a defensive position at a bridge that Orgonez would have to cross if he hoped to defeat them. Alvarado's troops also defended a ford at another point in the river, where Orgonez might try a flanking movement.

Alvarado's forces seemed to occupy a very strong position. But their defenses were about to be undermined. Pedro de Lerma, one of the soldiers in Alvarado's army, was secretly in league with Orgonez. He told the general of Alvarado's plans, suggesting that he send a force led by Orgonez across the ford in the darkness. When Alvarado rushed most of his troops against this attack, Almagro could then assault the bridge with the rest of his army. The trick worked. Alvarado's army was defeated.[9]

Almagro now felt strong enough to march west and confront his old enemy, Francisco Pizarro. Meanwhile, Pizarro had been reinforced. While the Inca had been besieging Cuzco the year before, Pizarro had called on the Spanish governors in Panama and Guatemala to help him. Finally, additional soldiers had arrived. In fact, Pizarro had begun marching with them from Lima toward Cuzco, only to learn that his brothers had been imprisoned and his relief force beaten. He then retreated to Lima to wait for Almagro there.

The Final Conflict

As Almagro prepared to leave Cuzco, Orgonez once again advised him to execute the two Pizarro brothers. Instead, Almagro decided to leave Gonzalo under arrest at the capital, where he soon got away from his captors and escaped to Lima. Hernando was forced to march with Almagro as a hostage. When the armies approached each other, Pizarro and Almagro—both now over sixty-five—met on November 13, 1537. They would try to resolve their differences. But the meeting immediately broke down into a terrible argument. Fearing that Almagro might execute his brother, Pizarro finally agreed to let his former partner hold on to Cuzco until the Spanish government could decide who should be the rightful governor of the capital. In return, Almagro would release Hernando, who would leave for Spain. When Almagro accepted these terms, Orgonez was convinced that his commander had made a terrible mistake that would cost all of them their lives. "What has my fidelity to my commander cost me!" he reportedly said.[10] Orgonez feared that the Pizarros would eventually kill Almagro and his men.

Orgonez was right. Once Hernando was released, Francisco Pizarro prepared his army to march against Almagro. Orgonez was supposed to fortify the mountain passes and prevent Pizarro's troops from marching eastward. He failed in his assignment. Pizarro's army, led by Hernando and Gonzalo, easily advanced across the mountains toward Cuzco.

On April 26, 1538, the two armies met in a huge struggle at Las Salinas, near the capital. Orgonez had drawn up his army of approximately five hundred soldiers behind a marsh and a stream, which he hoped would be a strong defensive position. His infantry had been placed in the center, with cavalry on each side to

Pizarro and Almagro, who had become enemies through their years in competition to conquer Peru, tried unsuccessfully to make peace.

drive off the enemy. He also had several small cannons to support his infantry.

With flags flying, Gonzalo Pizarro advanced toward the enemy, leading his infantry against the center of Orgonez's line. With approximately two hundred more men than the defenders, the Pizarros had an advantage. But Gonzalo found that, after crossing the stream, his assault was stoutly resisted by the enemy. The cannons Orgonez had placed on his flank raked the advancing soldiers, wreaking havoc among them. Gonzalo refused to retreat. His armored conquistadors pummeled the enemy with their swords, lances, and muskets, pushing them backward. While this struggle was under way, Hernando led his cavalry across the river. There, they clashed with the charging horsemen of Orgonez.

Orgonez was hit by a bullet. Then his horse was killed. Although he continued to fight valiantly, he, too, was eventually killed. His soldiers, who had been gradually giving up ground, now began fleeing the battlefield. This left the road open for the Pizarros to enter Cuzco. Throughout the battle, thousands of Inca had watched from the sidelines. They were interested to see which side might win. Now that the struggle was over, they robbed the corpses that lay on the battlefield.[11]

Once Hernando and Gonzalo reached Cuzco, they took Almagro prisoner. Hernando assured the old conquistador that he would be released after Francisco Pizarro arrived at Cuzco. But Hernando was actually planning something far different. Hernando collected evidence showing that Almagro had committed treason. Like Atahualpa before him, he was found guilty by a panel of judges and sentenced to death. Almagro pleaded with Hernando to show mercy. He could not believe that this should be his fate "for having spared your life so recently and under similar circumstances, when my advisers urged again and again that I should not spare you." But Hernando had no intention of saving the life of the man he hated. "Your fate is inevitable [already determined] and you may as well face it," he said.[12]

Almagro was executed. The Pizarros were now in complete control of Peru.

The Last Pizarro

Francisco Pizarro rode into Cuzco in 1539 to the sound of trumpets. At last, he was triumphant—the unchallenged leader of Peru. Pizarro wasted no time in rewarding his supporters. They received all the lands and possessions that had belonged to Almagro's men, who were left with nothing. Almagro's son, Diego, was supposed to inherit his father's dominions in Chile. But Pizarro refused to honor these claims. This angered Diego de Alvarado, who was supposed to govern these territories until the younger Almagro was old enough to govern them himself. But perhaps the eighteen-year-old Diego felt fortunate that he was not executed like his father. Instead, he was allowed to live in a house in Lima near the governor's palace, where Pizarro held court and ran the colony.

Pizarro sent his brother Hernando to Spain, bearing a large fortune in gold and silver for the king. Before leaving, Hernando warned Pizarro to be careful lest some of Almagro's supporters try to assassinate him:

> Let your Lordship make friends . . . giving sustenance [support] to whose who wish it, and do not permit those who wish nothing to assemble ten together within fifty leagues of wherever your Lordship may be, for if you let them assemble, they are bound to kill you.[1]

On the day that Hernando departed for Spain, neither brother could possibly know that this would be the last time they would ever see each other. News of Hernando's role in the death of Almagro had already reached the king's court. Alvarado had reached Spain before Hernando. There, he told the Spanish king's counselors that the Pizarros had decided not to honor the agreements that made Almagro's son the governor of Chile. Instead of the warm reception Hernando had hoped for, he was thrown into prison. He remained there for twenty years.

Francisco Pizarro returned to Lima. There, he continued his efforts to enlarge the city and attract more Spanish settlers to Peru. Some of the new colonists were sent eastward into the interior to live at small defensive posts, which Pizarro was setting up to protect the countryside. Manco, the last Incan ruler, had not stopped his attacks on the Spanish settlements. His guerrilla bands regularly swooped down from their mountain strongholds to burn a farm or plantation and kill its inhabitants. Manco was not prepared to give up control of Peru to the Spaniards.

Meanwhile, Pizarro also had to deal with another threat to his leadership. Almagro's supporters had never forgiven him for allowing their leader to be executed. They vowed revenge. A number of plans to assassinate Francisco Pizarro were discussed. The conspirators were led by Juan de Herrada (known as de Rada), a cavalier in Almagro's army and now the chief counselor to Almagro's son, Diego. Finally, the conspirators decided on a bold strategy that involved attacking Pizarro as he left the cathedral on the plaza after Sunday mass. June 26, 1541, was the day designated for the assassination.

As the day approached, one of the conspirators became frightened. He confessed the plan to a priest, who immediately reported the information to Pizarro's secretary. At first, Pizarro scoffed at the idea that anyone would try to assassinate him. Unwilling to take any needless chances, however, he stayed home that Sunday and met with some of the colony's officials at the palace.

When the conspirators realized what had happened, some of them were afraid of being arrested and wanted to leave Lima. But de Rada would not back down. Instead, he led a band of assassins to kill Pizarro. Yelling "Death to traitors," they made their way to the palace.[2] One of Pizarro's servants saw the conspirators and began yelling that the palace was under attack. Because most of the officials who were meeting with Pizarro were unarmed, they scrambled out the windows and left the palace.

Pizarro remained behind, along with his half brother Martín de Alcántara and a few soldiers. When he realized what was happening, Pizarro ordered one of the soldiers, Francisco de Chaves, to lock the heavy door to his private rooms so the conspirators could not enter. But the order was never carried out. Instead, Chaves stepped outside, where he was quickly overwhelmed and killed by the assassins. As they entered Pizarro's rooms, Alcantara engaged the assassins in fierce hand-to-hand combat. But they were too much for him. Pizarro himself entered the melee, yelling, ". . . traitors! Have you come to kill me in my own house?"[3] Almost seventy, he was still strong enough to hold off his assassins. But eventually, one of them wounded him, and as he fell, the others thrust their swords into his body.

A New Leader

The conspirators, led by de Rada, ran out of the palace, proclaiming that they had killed Pizarro. The dead conquistador would later be buried in a corner of the cathedral in Lima. Now that Francisco Pizarro was dead, the conspirators wanted Diego de Almagro to take his place.

Unknown to the conspirators, however, the Spanish king had already chosen a different governor for Peru. Charles V had sent a judge named Cristóbal Vaca de Castro to investigate the civil war that had been raging in Peru. Vaca de Castro had also been told that, if anything should happen to Pizarro, he should

Francisco Pizarro was assassinated after a civil war broke out between different factions of the Spanish conquistadors.

become the new governor. Charles V was growing tired of leaving Peru in the hands of unruly conquistadors. He believed the time had come to assert more direct control from Spain.

No sooner had Vaca de Castro arrived in South America, than he had to confront a very difficult situation. Not only was Pizarro dead, but a new civil war was about to begin. Although Diego de Almagro had been recognized as the new governor in parts of Peru, some of Pizarro's generals were not ready to follow him. When they heard that Vaca de Castro had the power to assume the governorship of Peru, they gave him their support.

Almagro and his chief counselor, de Rada, now found themselves at the head of an army in Lima that was being threatened by forces closing in on them from the north and the east. At first, Almagro hoped that he might be able to defeat each of these armies individually before they came together under Vaca de Castro's command. But de Rada died suddenly of a fever, leaving Almagro without his main advisor. To make matters even worse, two of his leading generals were feuding with each other. By the time this problem was solved, it was too late to do anything but retreat eastward toward Cuzco, escaping Vaca de Castro's superior army.

Almagro established a base of operations outside Cuzco and strengthened his forces for the coming battle. He gathered about five hundred soldiers, cavalry, and musketeers, as well as infantry carrying long pikes (spears). He also had a battery of artillery, which would give him additional fire power against Vaca de Castro. In addition, Almagro could count on the support of several thousand Inca warriors led by Manco, who wanted to see the Spanish authorities driven from Peru.

On September 16, 1542, Almagro's forces were on the plains of Chupas, about halfway between Cuzco and Lima. It was already late in the afternoon when Vaca de Castro's army appeared in front of them. But instead of camping for the night, Vaca de Castro decided to begin the attack immediately. His forces included about seven hundred troops, but very little artillery. Almagro had placed his artillery in the center of his line, supporting it with infantry and cavalry. As he had hoped, the big guns devastated the ranks of the enemy as they advanced against him.

Vaca de Castro's generals then tried to flank Almagro's position but ran into an assault from Manco's Indians, who were holding this part of the battle line. With volleys from their muskets, Vaca de Castro's men forced the Inca to retreat.

Meanwhile, the infantry regrouped and began another attack against Almagro's artillery. Across the plain, masses of enemy horsemen charged, using heavy lances or steel swords to hack at each other. It was a fierce clash that seesawed back and forth. Finally, Vaca de Castro charged with a force of cavalry that he had been holding in reserve. In the darkness, his forces drove Almagro from the field.

He was later captured by Vaca de Castro's men and executed at Cuzco.[4]

Another Governor for Peru

Following the defeat of Almagro, Governor Vaca de Castro expected that he would be given an opportunity to bring peace to Peru. But barely a year passed before the Spanish government decided to send someone to take his place.

Spain had passed a series of new laws relating to the colony. They were primarily aimed at improving the lives of the Indians, many of whom had been enslaved by the conquistadors and forced to work on farms and in mines. The Indians were to be freed upon the death of the current land owners. However, any conquistador who had abused the Indians or who had taken part in the civil wars would be forced to free them immediately. To carry out these laws, the Spanish government appointed a new viceroy—or supreme governor. His name was Blasco Núñez Vela.

The new laws struck at the heart of the Spaniards' economic system in Peru, which was dependent on Indian slave labor. The conquistadors, most of whom had fought for either Almagro or Pizarro, were afraid of losing their livelihoods. Many of them vowed to defy the laws.

Vela was in no mood to accept any opposition to his commands. He demanded complete obedience from the conquistadors. But the conquistadors believed that, since they had conquered the land, they had a right to run it the way they liked. In looking for someone who could lead them in this struggle, they turned to a man who possessed both the military experience and the boldness necessary to oppose the Spanish government successfully—Gonzalo Pizarro.

Gonzalo Pizarro Assumes Leadership

During the plot that ended in the assassination of his brother, Gonzalo had been far away from Lima, exploring the interior of the South American continent. By the time Gonzalo returned, his brother was dead. Although he offered his services to Vaca de Castro in the struggle against Almagro, the governor felt there was no significant role Gonzalo could play. Once the conquistadors began to express their dissatisfaction with the new laws enacted by Spain, however, Gonzalo believed the time had come for him to step in and claim his right as the last surviving Pizarro brother in Peru. As Vela entered Lima, Gonzalo was already building his own army in Cuzco.

The new viceroy tried to negotiate with Gonzalo to prevent a conflict, but Pizarro refused. Vela then began to strengthen his army so he could defeat Gonzalo on the battlefield. But this battle never occurred. Before the viceroy could march out of Lima, some of his own assistants arrested him to prevent another civil war. They established a new government, stating that the laws regarding slavery would not be enforced. Vela was sent back to Spain. They asked

Gonzalo, who was already approaching Lima, to send his army home.

But Gonzalo Pizarro believed that he had a right to assume the position of leadership that had been filled by his brother. With his army behind him, he entered Lima on October 28, 1544, and took control of the colony.

The Last Pizarro

Gonzalo Pizarro's decision meant that Peru had now declared its independence from Spain. In the sixteenth century, when governments were ruled by absolute monarchs, independence movements were not permitted. Charles V had no intention of allowing Gonzalo Pizarro to operate outside the control of Spain. But unless the monarch could gain the support of the Spanish conquistadors in the Americas and put a new army in the field, there seemed to be no way to stop Pizarro.

One man, however, did try to stop him. Instead of returning to Spain, Blasco Núñez Vela decided to remain in South America. As the only legitimate representative of the king, the viceroy hoped to build an army of loyal supporters who might eventually be strong enough to overthrow Pizarro. Establishing a base in the northern part of the colony, Vela struggled to create a fighting force. But the viceroy was not very popular. He could never gather the number of quality soldiers that served with Pizarro.

After a series of maneuvers, Pizarro and Vela finally gathered their armies for battle on January 18, 1546. Before the conflict began, Vela tried to encourage his men to fight bravely. He told them: "You are all brave men . . . and loyal to your sovereign . . . we are fighting for the right; it is the cause of God—the cause of God."[5]

It was no use. Pizarro's cavalry overwhelmed the viceroy's men in a massive cavalry battle. Vela was killed on the battlefield. Gonzalo Pizarro was now the master of Peru. In Lima, Spaniards hailed him as their "liberator" and "protector." Along the coast, one of his strongest supporters, Pedro de Hinojosa, commanded the ships controlling the sea lanes so that no one could land in Peru from Spain to lead another revolt against Pizarro.

While Pizarro was consolidating his conquests, the Spanish government was not idle. It decided to send a new envoy to Peru. He was a priest and talented administrator named Pedro de Gasca. Unlike the bull-headed Vela, Gasca was skilled at the art of negotiation. To help him negotiate with the leaders of the revolt in Peru, the government had authorized Gasca to offer a full pardon to anyone who would swear allegiance to the Spanish Crown. The new envoy came with no army, only a desire to end the conflict in the colony. Many of the conquistadors who had joined Gonzalo Pizarro did not like the idea of being in rebellion against their monarch. They also feared that

Spain had the power to punish rebels, just as Almagro had been punished.

Gradually, Gasca began to win over Pizarro's followers. By the end of 1546, Hinojosa had turned over the fleet to the Spanish envoy and accepted a full pardon for himself and his men. Meanwhile, Cuzco had also been taken over by forces loyal to the Spanish Crown. Gasca offered a pardon to Pizarro, but he refused. Instead, he raised a well-trained army in Lima, which remained loyal to him. But Gasca's ships were taking control of the coastline. It seemed only a matter of time before he would lead an army to attack Lima.

Eventually, Pizarro decided to leave Lima and march inland, hoping to find refuge. Soldiers were already deserting his army, and he might not have the strength to oppose Gasca. To make this journey, however, he had to defeat the army that had taken control of Cuzco. Although Pizarro's force was smaller, he had a well-trained corps of musketeers led by his second-in-command, Francisco de Carbajal. Over seventy, Carbajal had supported Pizarro's revolt against Vela and helped consolidate his power after the viceroy's defeat.

On October 26, 1547, Carbajal's musketeers were drawn up with the rest of Pizarro's army near the shores of Lake Titicaca. Before the battle, Carbajal told his men to aim carefully: "Remember, gentlemen, that the shot that goes high, even if it's only two inches over the enemy's head, is a wasted shot. . . . it's an advantage to hit the enemy in the thigh and legs, for it's a miracle if a man with [a] . . . wound there stands on his feet."[6]

The musketeers held their fire until the enemy infantry was only a short distance away. Then they unleashed a murderous volley that sent the enemy staggering backward. However, Gonzalo Pizarro's cavalry had not been so successful. It had been pushed back under a furious attack, and the enemy horsemen now charged Carbajal's position. Once again, the old conquistador proved more than a match for the enemy. Eventually, they fled the field. Pizarro was completely victorious.

The Last Battle

Instead of going to Chile, Pizarro now decided to make his headquarters at Cuzco. Garcilaso de la Vega, who was there at the time, said Pizarro was received like a hero:

> On his entry the bells of the cathedral and convents were rung. . . . The Indians in the city appeared in the square from their various quarters . . . and acclaimed him with loud shouts, calling him Inca and giving him other royal titles which they used in the triumphs of their own kings.[7]

While his army rested there, Pedro de Gasca led his forces eastward for the battle that would decide the future of the Spanish empire in Peru. His soldiers advanced slowly, threading their way through the narrow pathways of the high Andes. Pizarro had destroyed the bridges over the rivers, so these had to be rebuilt by Gasca's engineers. If Pizarro had also decided to defend the river crossings strongly, he might have prevented Gasca from reaching Cuzco for many months. Carbajal even offered to take a group of soldiers and contest one of the river crossings, but Pizarro felt he was far too valuable. "I need you near me . . . ," he said.[8] Instead, he sent another commander, Juan de

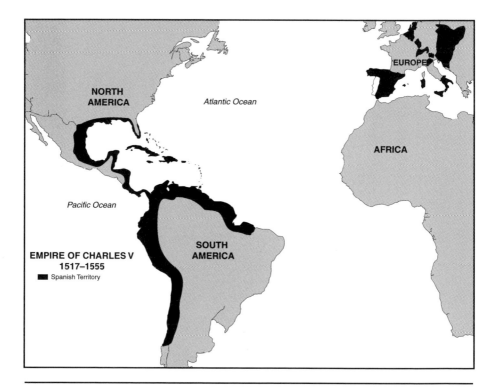

Spanish King Charles V held claim to an enormous empire in the New World in the mid-sixteenth century, thanks to the efforts of conquistadors like Cortés and Pizarro.

Acosta, who failed to stop Gasca's advance across the river.

The Spanish royal army, which numbered about two thousand well-equipped soldiers, arrived near Cuzco in April 1548. Marching into a broad valley, they spotted Pizarro's camp at the other end. Gasca drew up his soldiers into a battle line, with the infantry in the center and the cavalry on the flanks. Pizarro's army was only about half the size of his enemy's, but he hoped that his musketeers would once again bring him victory. As his soldiers prepared to meet the royal army, he rode among them and encouraged his outnumbered veterans to defeat the enemy. But when Pizarro's men saw the size of the army arrayed against them, they began to have second thoughts. Before the battle had even started, some of his cavalry and infantry had switched sides and defected to Gasca. The rest of his army, realizing that they were far too weak to win, ran from the battlefield. Pizarro now had no choice but to surrender.

When asked by Gasca why he had not been willing to swear allegiance to the Spanish Crown and avoid so many deaths, Pizarro told him that, since his family had conquered Peru, "as their representative here, I felt I had a right to the government."[9] This upset Gasca, who said: "Take him away; take him away. He's as much of a rebel today as he was yesterday."[10]

Pizarro was taken to Cuzco. Because of his rebellion against the Spanish Crown, he was executed. Spain now took complete control of the colony.

Chapter 8

Pizarro in Perspective

Francisco Pizarro, along with his brothers and their fellow conquistadors, introduced a new culture to Peru—one that has shaped the country ever since. They introduced the Spanish language, the Catholic religion, and a government run by soldiers. They also carried terrible weapons of destruction, such as the musket and the cannon, as well as new technology, such as the wheel and the sailing ship. With these ships, Peru became part of a transatlantic empire, ruled by Spain.

Pizarro established a great city at Lima, which became the center of all the Spanish colonies in South America. Many Spanish settlers followed Pizarro to Lima and to the other towns that were developed in Peru. Some of them intermarried with the Inca. Garcilaso de la Vega, for example, was the son of a Spanish conquistador and an Incan princess.

Most of the Incan people, however, were reduced to second-class status. They were expected to pay tribute to the Spanish conquerors and work on the large Spanish farms, called *haciendas*. Although slavery was officially banned in Spanish America, the Indians were usually paid so poorly for their work on the haciendas that they were little more than slaves.

Meanwhile, many of the Indians were stricken with diseases brought by the Spanish to the Americas. In fact, an estimated 40 percent of the Indian population died from outbreaks of measles, smallpox, and other illnesses that had been unknown to them before the arrival of the Spaniards.[1]

In the centuries since the Spanish conquest of Peru, the nation has often been ruled by the military.

GRATVS ET

TVGRATIS

Francisco Pizarro, the great Spanish conquistador, is often viewed
negatively for the terrible effects he had on the native people of Peru.

Other Indians were forced to dig in the mines. Silver had been mined by the Inca, and the mining increased after the Spanish conquest. At rich silver veins, such as Potosi in upper Peru, more than ten thousand Indians were brought together to do the back-breaking work of digging out vast loads of silver. Much of it was then transported to Lima and shipped back to Spain. This silver helped pay the armies that made Spain the greatest power in Europe during the sixteenth and seventeenth centuries.

By the eighteenth century, however, Spain had already entered a long decline. The supply of silver had decreased. Spain had also spent too much money trying to extend its power in Europe. The Spanish government no longer had the strength to hold its vast empire together. During the 1820s, a rebellion led by Generals José de San Martín and Simón Bolívar enabled Peru and the other Spanish colonies in South America to achieve their independence. Throughout the rest of the nineteenth century, Peru was frequently ruled by military dictators. Ever since Pizarro's conquest of Peru, military rule seemed to be a natural form of government.

During the twentieth century, Peru continued to be governed by a series of dictators, with brief periods of liberal government. Although efforts have been made at times to improve the position of the Indians, they remain impoverished—a direct legacy of the Spanish conquest.

1200—The Inca build their empire in Peru.

1440—Pachacuti Inca Yupanqui and Topa Inca Yupanqui expand the empire until it becomes known as the four quarters of the world.

ca. **1471**—Francisco Pizarro is born in Trujillo, Spain.

1492—Columbus sails for America.

1509—Pizarro sails for America.

1510—Pizarro has his first independent command.

1513—Pizarro accompanies Balboa to the Pacific Ocean.

1519—Hernando Cortés begins his conquest of Mexico.

1524—Pizarro leads his first expedition to Peru.

1525—Huayna Capac, the last great Incan king, dies; Civil war breaks out in Incan Empire.

1526—Pizarro draws his famous "line in the sand."

1528—Pizarro returns to Spain to get support for his expedition.

1531—Pizarro begins his last voyage to Peru.

1532—Pizarro enters Cajamarca; He captures the Incan king, Atahualpa.

1533—Atahualpa is executed.

1535—Pizarro establishes the new city of Lima.

1536—Spanish withstand a six-month siege by the Inca at Cuzco.

1538—Pizarro defeats and executes his partner Almagro.

1541—Pizarro is assassinated.

1544—Gonzalo Pizarro takes control of Peru.

1548—Gonzalo Pizarro is executed; Spain reasserts control of Peru.

1824—Simón Bolívar liberates Peru from Spanish rule.

Chapter Notes

Chapter 1. A Line in the Sand

1. William H. Prescott, *History of the Conquest of Mexico and History of the Conquest of Peru* (New York: Random House, 1989), pp. 853–854.

2. Ibid., p. 860.

3. Cecil Howard, *Pizarro and the Conquest of Peru* (New York: American Heritage, 1968), p. 21.

Chapter 2. The Making of a Conquistador

1. Alan Lloyd, *The Spanish Centuries* (New York: Doubleday, 1968), p. 73.

2. Henry Steele Commager, ed., "Privileges and Prerogatives Granted to Columbus, April 30, 1492," *Documents of American History* (New York: Appleton-Century-Crofts, Inc., 1958), vol. 1, p. 1.

3. Frank Shay, *Incredible Pizarro: Conqueror of Peru* (New York: Mohawk Press, 1932), pp. 15–17.

4. Ibid., p. 25.

5. Daniel J. Boorstin, *The Discoverers* (New York: Random House, 1983), p. 258.

6. Shay, pp. 77–78.

7. Bernal Diaz, "The Conquistadors Enter Mexico City, 8 November 1519," *The Mammoth Book of Eyewitness History*, ed. Jon E. Lewis (New York: Carroll & Graf Publishers, Inc., 1998), pp. 111–112.

8. Shay, p. 115.

Chapter 3. The Incan Empire

1. Garcilaso de la Vega, El Inca, *Royal Commentaries of the Incas, Part One* (Austin: University of Texas, 1966), pp. 180–181.

2. Garcilaso de la Vega, "The Incas' Golden Garden," *Eyewitness to History*, ed. John Carey (New York: Avon Books, 1987), p. 89.

3. De la Vega, *Royal Commentaries of the Incas, Part One*, p. 150.

4. Pedro de Cieza de León, *The Second Part of the Chronicle of Peru* (New York: Burt Franklin, 1883), p. 65.

5. Ibid., pp. 33, 57.

6. De la Vega, *Royal Commentaries of the Incas, Part One*, p. 246.

7. Pedro de Cieza de León, "Taxation of the Incas," *The Peru Reader: History, Culture, Politics,* eds. Orin Starn, Carlos Iván Degregori, and Robin Kirk (Durham, N.C.: Duke University Press, 1995), p. 71.

8. Ruth Karen, *Kingdom of the Sun—The Inca: Empire Builders of the Americas* (New York: Four Winds Press, 1975), p. 65.

9. Ibid., p. 8.

10. De la Vega, *Royal Commentaries of the Incas, Part One*, p. 279.

11. Cieza de León, *The Second Part of the Chronicle of Peru*, p. 68.

Chapter 4. The Conquest Begins

1. William H. Prescott, *History of the Conquest of Mexico and History of the Conquest of Peru* (New York: Random House, 1989), pp. 878–879.

2. Frank Shay, *Incredible Pizarro: Conqueror of Peru* (New York: Mohawk Press, 1932), p. 127.

3. Cecil Howard, *Pizarro and the Conquest of Peru* (New York: American Heritage, 1968), p. 62.

4. Prescott, p. 913.

5. Hernán Cortés, *Letters From Mexico*, trans. and ed. Anthony Pagden (New Haven, Conn.: Yale University Press, 1986), p. 39.

6. Shay, p. 172.

7. Garcilaso de la Vega, El Inca, *Royal Commentaries of the Incas, Part Two* (Austin: University of Texas Press, 1966), pp. 665–666.

8. Ibid., p. 667.

9. Shay, p. 180.

10. Clements R. Markham, ed., *Reports on the Discovery of Peru* (New York: Burt Franklin, 1970), p. 45.

11. Prescott, p. 930.

Chapter 5. Pizarro Lays a Trap

1. William H. Prescott, *History of the Conquest of Mexico and History of the Conquest of Peru* (New York: Random House, 1989), p. 938.

2. Garcilaso de la Vega, El Inca, *Royal Commentaries of the Incas, Part Two* (Austin: University of Texas Press, 1966), pp. 680–681.

3. Prescott, p. 942.

4. Ibid., pp. 947–948.

5. Ibid., p. 953.

6. Victor von Hagen, *The Royal Road of the Inca* (London: Gordon & Cremonesi, 1976), p. 50.

7. De la Vega, p. 696.

8. Prescott, p. 967.

9. Edwin Williamson, *The Penguin History of Latin America* (London: The Penguin Press, 1992), p. 26.

10. Cecil Howard, *Pizarro and the Conquest of Peru* (New York: Harper and Row, 1968), p. 93.

Chapter 6. Civil War

1. William H. Prescott, *History of the Conquest of Mexico and History of the Conquest of Peru* (New York: Random House, 1989), p. 1004.

2. Pedro Pizarro, *Relation of the Discovery and Conquest of the Kingdoms of Peru* (New York: The Cortes Society, 1921), vol. 1, pp. 300–301.

3. Prescott, p. 1020.

4. Pizarro, p. 301.

5. Ibid., pp. 310–315; Prescott, pp. 1026–1028.

6. Prescott, p. 1024.

7. Ibid., p. 1041.

8. Cecil Howard, *Pizarro and the Conquest of Peru* (New York: American Heritage, 1968), p. 110.

9. Frank Shay, *Incredible Pizarro* (New York: The Mohawk Press, 1932), pp. 283–284.

10. Howard, pp. 112–113.

11. Prescott, pp. 1054–1055.

12. Shay, p. 294.

Chapter 7. The Last Pizarro

1. Pedro Pizarro, *Relation of the Discovery and Conquest of the Kingdoms of Peru* (New York: The Cortes Society, 1921), vol. 1, p. 395.

2. Ibid., p. 421.

3. William H. Prescott, *History of the Conquest of Mexico and History of the Conquest of Peru* (New York: Random House, 1989), p. 1088.

4. Ibid., pp. 1109–1116.

5. Ibid., p. 1151.

6. Garcilaso de la Vega, El Inca, *Royal Commentaries of the Incas, Part Two* (Austin: University of Texas Press, 1966), p. 1141.

7. Ibid., p. 1163.

8. Ibid., p. 1175.

9. Prescott, p. 1210.

10. De la Vega, p. 1196.

Chapter 8. Pizarro in Perspective

1. Edwin Williamson, *The Penguin History of Latin America* (London: The Penguin Press, 1992), p. 87.

Further Reading

Books

Boorstin, Daniel J. *The Discoverers*. New York: Random House, 1983.

Dworkin, Mark J. *Mayas, Aztecs & Incas: Mysteries of Ancient Civilizations of Central & South America*. New York: DIANE Publishing Company, 1999.

Morrison, Marion. *Atahuallpa and the Incas*. New York: The Bookwright Press, 1986.

Prescott, William H. *History of the Conquest of Mexico and History of the Conquest of Peru*. New York: Random House, 1989.

Stern, Steve J. *Peru's Indian Peoples and the Challenge of Spanish Conquest*. Madison: University of Wisconsin Press, 1982.

Von Hagen, Victor. *The Incas: People of the Sun*. Cleveland: World Publishing, 1961.

Internet Addresses

Halsall, Paul. "Pedro de Cieza de Léon: Chronicles of the Incas, 1540." *Modern History Sourcebook*. July 1998. <http://www.fordham.edu/halsall/mod/1540cieza.html> (September 24, 1999).

Jacobs, James Q. *Tupac Amaru: The Life, Times and Execution of the Last Inca*. 1998. <http://www.geocities.com/Athens/Olympus/4844/tupac_amaru.html> (September 24, 1999).

University of Pennsylvania Library. *Cultural Readings: Colonization & Print in the Americas*. September 21, 1998. <http://www.library.upenn.edu/special/gallery/kislak/index/cultural.html> (September 24, 1999).

Index